Exousia, Your God Given Authority

By Donald Peart

Acknowledgments

I honor and thank our Lord Jesus Christ who has been given "all authority … in heaven and on earth."

Table of Contents

Introduction

Contrary to popular belief Jesus is the person in charge. Most in the Church speaks more about the devil than they do about Jesus' authority and the authority He has given to His Church. Also, many in the world have no concept that the world is technically influenced by spiritual entities. The world was once given to Adam to dominate. Adam was given authority on the earth and over the earth. However, through transgression, the world became more influenced by a spirit serpent rather than mankind. Then came the time when dominion (authority) was restored to man. The Man, Jesus, came and judged the world by casting out the prince of the world. Jesus was also given "'every' authority" in heaven and on the earth; and He restored dominion over sin, death, and all spirits to His Church.

Jesus did indeed put **all things** in subjection to Himself; and God put all things in subjection to mankind in general. Yet, we know by experience and by the record of the Scriptures that "we do not see all things put under [mankind]. But we see Jesus." Yes, Jesus is the King of heaven, King of the earth, the kingdom of the world belongs to Jesus and all who dwell therein. It follows that we must follow the pattern of our Lord Jesus Christ to rule over "the things in world"[1] through Him. Jesus has all authority, and we flow under His authority if we remain in Him.

Note: we are not to rule in the world through fleshly violence;[2] we rule the world through "the authority of His Christ" by the Holy Spirit. That is, we walk and live in the **finish work**[3] of Jesus and rule in Him because His Spirit is in us! There is an "authority **of** His Christ" that we as believer must "put on" to walk **in** "the authority of His Christ." We do not have to be weaklings and crouch to the elements of the world. We are sons of God, **now,**

---

[1] Lust of the eyes, lust of the flesh and the ostentation of livelihood (I John 2:16)
[2] John 18:36
[3] John 19:30, Hebrews 10:12-13, John 16:11

through faith in Christ Jesus, through water baptism and through the baptism of the Holy Spirit. According to the Scriptures Jesus has redeemed us from the slavery of the elements of the world and "placed us as sons" into being "masters of all" principalities and powers in the heavenly realms.

Our dominion in the world is realized in the earth when we understand that the authority of His Christ is already established. We must realize that Jesus cast out the prince of this world, and the Father "delivered all things" into Jesus' hand. Jesus then told his disciples to go and disciple the nations after He established to them that He (Jesus) is given "'every' authority ... in heaven and on earth." We must also realize that Michael cast out the great dragon out of heaven.

We are to marginalize the Devil. The dragon has no more "place" in the heavens. Since Jesus cast the Devil out of the world, and Michael, the arch angel, cast Satan out of heaven; who is in charge now? Jesus is the Lord of all! The Devil has no more authority over any believer who has turned from the authority of Satan unto the authority of God. Satan has **"no place!"** The Holy Spirit of Jesus is the ruling Spirit in the earth and over the earth! **"The Kingdom of this world have become ... of our Lord and of His Christ and He shall reign forever and ever!"** We must now take the doctrine of Jesus authority and apply it to our lives. We have to live what we know and move beyond the abstract. We must now demonstrate the authority of Jesus, personally. We must "now" demonstrate "all that Jesus began **both** to **do** and **teach**," as Luke declared in Acts 1:1.

The Authority of His Christ

Revelation 12:10, NIV: Then I heard a loud voice in heaven say: "Now have come the salvation and the power and the kingdom of our God, and the authority of his Christ. For the accuser of our brothers, who accuses them before our God day and night, has been hurled down.

"The authority of His Christ" is an especially important truth; and it is critical that the Church of the Lord Jesus understands the meaning. With that said, to really appreciate the meaning of the phrase "**the authority** of His Christ" as it relates to Jesus and us, we must gain an understanding of who is "the Christ." There is Christ the head—Jesus; and there is Christ the many membered body of believers.

Matthew 16:13, NIV: When Jesus came to the region of Caesarea Philippi, he asked his disciples, "Who do people say the Son of Man is?"

Matthew 16:16-17, NIV: [16]Simon Peter answered, "You are the Christ, the Son of the living God." [17]Jesus replied, "Blessed are you, Simon son of Jonah, for this was not revealed to you by man, but by my Father in heaven.

There is no doubt in the Father's mind and in the mind of all true disciples that Jesus is the Christ. Jesus asked His disciple, **"Who do people say the Son of Man is?"** Peter received an answer by revelation from the Father—God, and declared; **"You are the Christ, the Son of the living God**." This is the truth; Jesus is the Christ, the Son of the living God. In fact, our rebirth into God's kingdom is predicated upon this truth as indicated by **1 John 5:1a: "Everyone who believes that Jesus is the Christ is born of God**."

Thus, the foundation of our salvation (rebirth) is to believe that Jesus is the Christ. No other persons or names have the power to birth us again into the kingdom of God. We are only born "out of" God when we believe that Jesus is the Christ! Here are some examples of believers who declared and believed that Jesus indeed the Christ.

John 11:27, NIV: "Yes, Lord," [Martha][4] told him, "I believe that you are the Christ, the Son of God, who was to come into the world."

John 20:30-31, NIV: [30]Jesus did many other miraculous signs in the presence of his disciples, which are not recorded in this book. [31]But these are written that you may believe that Jesus is the Christ, the Son of God, and that by believing you may have life in his name.

Acts 9:20: Immediately [Paul][5] preached the Christ in the synagogues, that He is the Son of God.

Now that we have seen that Jesus is the Christ, we must also understand that there is another aspect of the Christ that is not taught much. The Body of Christ is also considered as Christ. I first learned this aspect of Christ from Dr. Kelley Varner, my mentor for 16 years and who became as a father to me several years before his passing.

1 Corinthians 12:12-13: [12]For as the body is one and has many members, but all the members of that one body, being many, are one body, so also is Christ. [13]For by one Spirit we were all baptized into one body—whether Jews or Greeks, whether slaves or free—and have all been made to drink into one Spirit.

Did you hear what you just read! Christ is now "one" body of believer made up of many members. There is Jesus, "the Christ"— the Head of the Body; and there is Christ—Jesus' body of believer made up of many members. The "Head" (Jesus, the Christ) and His body of many members (corporate Christ) are now "one."

Yes, if you have been baptized into the one Body of Christ by the "one Spirit," you are now a part of Christ. "For as the body is **one** and has many members, but all the members of that one body, being many, are one body, **so also is Christ.** For by **one Spirit,** we

---

[4] Inserted by this author to identify the person the Scripture is referencing
[5] Inserted by this author to identify the person the Scripture is referencing

were all **baptized** into **one** body." Here is more proof from the apostle Paul.

Galatians 3:27-28: 27For as many of you as were baptized into Christ have put on Christ. 28There is neither Jew nor Greek, there is neither slave nor free, there is neither male nor female; for you are all one in Christ Jesus.

Paul gave another witness that the true Church is also considered as Christ. Once we are baptized into Christ we have put on Christ. Whenever, I put on a coat that coat covers me, my body is no longer seen; the coat is now seen. It follows that when I put on Christ by baptism of the "one Spirit," people will see who I am covered with. Christ is now seen on me and is "in" me and I am in Him. I should no longer be seen; Christ is now seen because I have put on Christ by the baptism of the one Spirit. "There is neither Jew nor Greek, there is neither slave nor free, there is neither male nor female; **for you are all one in Christ Jesus.**"

When you are baptized into the "many membered" Body of Christ, if you are a Jew, you are no longer distinguished as a Jew, if you are a Gentile, you are no longer distinguished as a Gentile, if you are a male, you are no longer seen as just a mare man, and if you are a female you are no longer perceived as lesser, if a slave no longer just a slave, if free, no longer a freeman, **"you are all one in Christ!"** Why?

By baptism, you have "put on Christ;" and if you can receive it, as Paul taught, you who are now baptized into Jesus' Body of many ethnicities are "also … Christ." Christ is now a corporate entity — Jesus, the Christ is the Head of the Body, and His Church corporately is also Christ through baptism of His Holy Spirit into one Body. Therefore, if you have received that the Church of Jesus Christ is also considered as Christ; then we can now discuss "the authority of His Christ."

Colossians 2:9-10: ⁹For in Him dwells all the fullness of the Godhead bodily; ¹⁰and you are complete in Him, who is the head of all principality and power.

The verses above are interesting verses, especially verse ten. That is, the verses above are powerful as translated by New King James from the Greek text. However, the literal rendition of verse ten (Colossians 2:10) above is very enlightening (I am not sure why the translators did not translate this verse exactly as the Greek reads). **Here is how Colossians 2:10 literally reads:**

Colossians 2:10: "And you are in Him having been filled who is the Head of all principalities and authorities."

Thus, according to Paul, we are "in" Jesus because we are "filled" with Christ, our Lord ("now the Lord is the Spirit"[6]). If we are "in Him" then Jesus clothes us. Jesus is "in" us; and we are also "in Him" by the same Spirit. Paul then continued by saying that Jesus is the Head of all principalities and authorities; thus, it is also true that as long as we are "in Him," we can also walk in Jesus' authority (His headship) as Christ. However, I must emphasize that "the authority of His Christ" is only realized in Jesus as He has exercised His authority given to Him by the Father.

Since "the authority" belong to "His Christ." Then, we must learn the context of Jesus' authority for this same authority to work in and through us. The phrase "His Christ" is translated three times in the New Testament, and one time in the Old Testament, as such. It is used once by the apostle Peter in the book of Acts, twice by the beloved apostle John in the book of Revelation, and once in Psalms, chapter 2.

Acts 4:26: The kings of the earth took their stand, and the rulers were gathered together against the LORD and against His Christ.

---

[6] 2 Corinthians 3:17

Revelation 11:15: Then the seventh angel sounded: And there were loud voices in heaven, saying, "The kingdoms of this world have become the kingdoms of our Lord and of His Christ, and He shall reign forever and ever!"

Revelation 12:7-10: [7]And there was war in heaven. Michael and his angels fought against the dragon, and the dragon and his angels fought back. [8]But he was not strong enough, and they lost their place in heaven. [9]The great dragon was hurled down-- that ancient serpent called the devil, or Satan, who leads the whole world astray. He was hurled to the earth, and his angels with him. [10]Then I heard a loud voice in heaven say: "Now have come the salvation and the power and the kingdom of our God, and the authority of his Christ. For the accuser of our brothers, who accuses them before our God day and night, has been hurled down.

Psalm 2:1-3: [1]Why do the nations rage, and the people plot a vain thing? [2]The kings of the earth set themselves, and the rulers take counsel together, against the LORD and against His Anointed, saying, [3]"Let us break their bonds in pieces and cast away Their cords from us."

In the book of Acts 4, Peter and some of the apostles and saints were being held and persecuted for a notable miracle that Peter and John performed. Eventually, the Sanhedrin council attempted to forbid the apostles from speaking in the name of Jesus. Once, the apostles were released Peter and the saints began to pray. In the prayer Peter indicated that "the rulers were gathered together Against **the LORD** and against **His Christ**." Peter then identified "the Lord" and "His Christ" as he continued to pray.

Peter said, [27]"For truly **against Your holy Servant Jesus,** whom You anointed, both Herod and Pontius Pilate, with the Gentiles and the people of Israel, were gathered together [28]to do whatever Your hand and Your purpose determined before to be done. [29]**Now, Lord, look on their threats,** and grant to **Your servants** that with all boldness they may speak Your word" **(Acts 4:27-29).**

In these verses (Acts 4:27-29) Peter mentioned the Lord Jesus Christ as the one whom the rulers were "against;' and Peter also included the believers ("your **servants**") in the "threats" they had received from the Sanhedrin. Thus, Peter included Jesus, the Christ, and the believers with him. This truth is borne out in Psalm 2 as we will discuss in a moment. That is, the Lord is Jesus and "His Christ" is Jesus and the body of believers, as one. Peter included himself and those whom he was praying with as "His Christ." Yes, Jesus is both Lord and Christ. Yet, as we saw earlier in 1 Corinthians 12:12, "Christ" is also the Body of believers who are baptized into the Christ. Did you know that Jesus identified His Church as Himself?

Acts 9:1-4: [1]Then Saul, still breathing threats and murder against the disciples of the Lord, went to the high priest, [2]and asked letters from him to the synagogues of Damascus, so that if he found any who were of the Way, whether men or women, he might bring them bound to Jerusalem. [3]As he journeyed he came near Damascus, and suddenly a light shone around him from heaven. [4]Then he fell to the ground, and heard a voice saying to him, "Saul, Saul, why are you persecuting Me?"

In the reference above Saul (before he was converted by Jesus) was persecuting the Church of Jesus. So, Jesus paid Saul a personal visit. As Jesus introduced Himself to Saul (Paul), Jesus did not say to Saul, why are you persecuting My Church? On the contrary, Jesus identified His Church, as Himself. Jesus said, "Saul, Saul, why are you persecuting **Me?" Jesus** equated **His Church** to **Himself! The Church is Mrs. Jesus. Just as Jesus is the Christ, the Father as so seen fit to call the Church "His Christ."**

"His Christ" is also used in Revelation 11:15 after the seventh angel sounded the seventh trumpet. After this trumpet was sounded, it was declared that the kingdom of the world has become **"of"** the Lord and **"of"** His Christ. Yes! The kingdom of the world is become **of** our Lord and of His Christ. As we will see later, the kingdom of the world was conquered by Jesus during His life and the conquest was ratified at the cross.

We must walk in this same authority that Jesus walked in, is walking in and shall walk in with respect to overcoming the world. In Jesus' authority, we now exercise the authority of His Christ in the world. Satan does not own the world! Jesus owns the world. In

Luke 10, Jesus declared that all things were delivered to Him of His Father!

"His Christ" is also used in Revelation 12:10; and in this verse, it explains when "the authority of His Christ" is come. That is, an event occurred in the heavens which caused a declaration to be made that "the authority of His Christ" is come. Here is the account of the event. A war broke out in heaven. Michael and his angel fought against the dragon and his angel.

The dragon was defeated and cast out of heaven to the earth. Upon this truth (Satan being cast out of heaven), it was declared that "the authority of His Christ" is now come! "Then I heard a loud voice in heaven say**: "Now have come** … the authority of **his Christ**. **For the accuser of our brother … has been hurled down" (Revelation 12:10, NIV).**

Finally, in the book of Psalm the phrase "against the Lord and against His anointed" is also used. In this reference, it is obvious that David considered "the Lord and … His anointed (Christ)" as a corporate entity. That is, as already established, the Lord and his anointed are identified as **"their"** (plural) in the associated verses.

> "¹Why do the nations rage, and the people plot a vain thing? ²The kings of the earth set themselves, and the rulers take counsel together, against the LORD and against His Anointed, saying, ³"Let us break their bonds in pieces and cast away their cords from us" (Psalm 2:1-3).

The **"their"** (plural) is refereeing to "the Lord" and "His Christ." Thus, His Christ includes both "the Christ" (Jesus) and corporate Christ — Jesus' Church. We have seen that there is "the Christ." There is also "His Christ;" and there is "the authority of His Christ."

This "authority" is exercised in and over the kingdom of the world "now" when we understand that Jesus ejected the Devil out of the world. This authority of His Christ is exercised in the "now" when we understand that the great dragon has been ejected from heaven by Michael. Because we are filled with Jesus' Spirit, Jesus is now in us, and we are in Him! How can this be? He filled us, yet we are in Him. Yes, His Spirit cannot be contained in us! Know you not that God fills the heavens and the earth (Jeremiah 23:24). Thus, the Spirit of Jesus living in you also means that you are in Him; and if He is in you and you in Him, as He is the head of all principalities and authorities, so are you also able to exercise Jesus' authority.

The Kingdom of the World is the Lord's

Revelation 11:15: Then the seventh angel sounded: And there were loud voices in heaven, saying, "The kingdoms of this world have become the kingdoms of our Lord and of His Christ, and He shall reign forever and ever!"

Jesus reigns over the kingdom of the world. The former prince of the world (Satan) has been cast out of the world. The kingdoms of the world no longer belong to Satan. Yet, some in the Church have not known this truth. If we listen to some of our thoughts, speech, and action, it can appear that the Devil is in charge. However, Satan is not in charge. Jesus is in charge. Jesus is the authority!

The world no longer belongs to the Devil. Do you know that one of the purposes of the Holy Spirit being given to us is to convince us and to expose to us that the prince of this world (Satan) is already judged? Yes, Jesus judged Satan; and thus, we now have authority to exercise Jesus' judgments over Satan and his angels. Yes! We now have authority in the world and over the world.

John 12:28-33: [28]"Father, glorify Your name." Then a voice came from heaven, saying, "I have both glorified it and will glorify it again." [29]Therefore the people who stood by and heard it said that it had thundered. Others said, "An angel has spoken to Him." [30]Jesus answered and said, "This voice did not come because of Me, but for your sake. [31]"Now is the judgment of this world; now the ruler of this world will be cast out. [32]"And I, if I am lifted up from the earth, will draw all peoples to Myself." [33]This He said, signifying by what death He would die.

Jesus declared that "now," yes **now** is the judgment of this world; **now** the ruler of this world will be cast out." If approximately 2,000 years ago Jesus declared that the "now" existed against the prince of this world, it follows that the "now" that Jesus declared is also true today. The Church of Jesus needs to understand that "now" (right now) is the former prince of this world judged when Jesus cast him out of the world. Jesus finished His judgment against

Satan and His judgment against the world at the cross. Jesus came in the flesh; destroyed the works of the devil; and the Father delivered all things to Jesus.

At one time Satan indicated to Jesus that the kingdoms of the worlds were delivered to him (the Devil) and that he had authority to give it to whoever he chose. Also, Jesus did indeed say that there was a ruler of the world that He had to cast out this ruler. With that said, Satan no longer has legal authority over the world. Jesus now holds all authority in heaven and on earth.

Luke 4:5-8: 5Then the devil, taking Him up on a high mountain, showed Him all the kingdoms of the world in a moment of time. 6And the devil said to Him, "All this authority I will give You, and their glory; for this has been delivered to me, and I give it to whomever I wish. 7"Therefore, if You will worship before me, all will be Yours." 8And Jesus answered and said to him, "Get behind Me, Satan! For it is written, 'You shall worship the LORD your God, and Him only you shall serve.'

We see above that the Devil showed Jesus all the kingdoms of the world and its "authority" in an attempt to have Jesus worship him. Jesus put Satan "behind" him (lit., "under" him); and cut Satan with the sword of His Word—Jesus declared **"You shall worship the LORD your God, and Him only you shall serve."** Jesus also corrected Satan's statement when Satan asserted that "the kingdoms of the world … this authority …has been **delivered** to me [Satan]."

Jesus countered Satan's assertion by declaring in Luke 10:22 that **"All things have been delivered to Me by My Father."** Jesus is the authority that "now" rules over the earth and the world. The Father delivered "all things" to the Son—Jesus, the Christ. The Church must now walk under Jesus' authority; and the Holy Spirit has been sent to convince us of this truth that the world and its former prince has been judged; and the world is now the Lord's and His Christ.

John 16:7-11: [7] Nevertheless I tell you the truth. It is to your advantage that I go away; for if I do not go away, the Helper will not come to you; but if I depart, I will send Him to you. [8] And when He has come, He will convict the world of sin, and of righteousness, and of judgment: [9] of sin, because they do not believe in Me; [10] of righteousness, because I go to My Father and you see Me no more; [11] of judgment, because the ruler of this world is judged.

Jesus declared in John 12:31 that **"Now is the judgment of this world; now the ruler of this world will be cast out."** **No**w is the world judged! **No**w is the ruler of this world judged! Yet, it will take the Helper (the Holy Spirit) to **"convict** the world … of judgment, **because** the **ruler of the world is judged."** We are supposed to know that the ruler of this world has been judged; and we are to allow the Holy Spirit in us to "convict" (expose, show light to correct) the world of this truth.

Jesus is the Head of all principalities and authorities on earth and in the heavenly; and we are in Him having been filled. Since we are in Him (in Christ Jesus) through the filling of the Helper (the Spirit), we also walk in the authority of Jesus' headship. The kingdom of the world has become the Lord's and His Christ! This is true now; and it is not just a future concept.

Revelation 11:15: Then the seventh angel sounded: And there were loud voices in heaven, saying, "The kingdoms of this world have become the kingdoms of our Lord and of His Christ, and He shall reign forever and ever!"

In the verse above, the "seventh angel 'trumpeted'." "Trumpeted" or "sounded" is in the aoristic tense. "The kingdoms of the world have **become** …." "Become" is also in the aoristic tense in the middle voice. Aoristic tense indicates an event that happened in the past with no limit on repetition or duration. That is, the event happened in the past with ongoing eternal repetition.

The angel sounded, the angel is sounding, and the angel shall sound. So, what did the angel trumpet and is trumpeting and shall trumpet? The seventh angel trumpeted that the kingdom of the world **became** our Lord's and His Christ. "And there were loud voices in heaven saying, 'the kingdoms of this world **have become** the kingdom of our Lord and His Christ, and he shall reign forever and ever!'"

Jesus cast Satan out of this world! Jesus judged the world. "All things" were delivered to Jesus. It follows that the kingdom of this world is now become of our Lord and His Christ. "Become" is in the "middle voice." This means that the subject performs the action upon himself/herself. In other word, the kingdom of the world became our Lord's and His Christ, not because they were forced. On the contrary, they became "of" our Lord and His Christ by performing this action upon themselves. Here are accounts of a blessing that was bestowed without force for the kingdom of the world is the Lord's.

It was my final year of engineering school. I became so frustrated with our financial situation relative to tuition for school (even though up to that time the Father was faithful with providing my tuition from semester to semester) and I was also frustrated with the little income we had coming in. I remember falling on my face on the living room floor and conversed with the Father stating that I am going to quit school; because I had no money for tuition and that I wanted to work two jobs to help my family's financial situation. The voice of the Lord came to me and said, "Get up and go to school and register."

I obeyed and went to school to do as He said. I arrived at school believing the word of the Lord. To my surprise, there was a block on my name, and I could not register. So, I went back home, which was forty minutes from the school, and fell on my face again in the same spot, saying, Lord You told me to go to the school and register, yet there was a block on my name, and I could not register. The voice of the Father came to me again, and said, "Go back to the school and register." To my surprise when I went back the second time, the block on my name was removed; and I was able to register.

Next, I had to get the money I needed for tuition. I then went to the engineering building; and to my surprise again, they were giving away money to students with certain criteria. I fit the criteria and received money for that year. The kingdom of the world is the Lord's; and without any force on my part, I registered and received the money to complete college. The world is the Lord's and His Christ's. The Scripture says that we are to uses the resources of the sea (of humanity).

In 1987 after returning from Japan my wife and I did not have the money to be able to move to North Carolina. It was not too long after that we saw Jesus example happened again. Jesus indicated that money could be found in fish mouth (Matthew 17:27). Jesus also said that His disciple would become "fishers of men" (Matthew 4:19). My wife and I prayed concerning the money we needed to move; and in a night vision I saw three vans drove up swiftly and came to a stop; as this occurred in the vision, I also heard that my brother would be saved and that he would give us the money we needed. (My brother also owned a home improvement company.

It is also worthy to note that during this time of need, my wife gave our last $40 to a pastor.) After the vision, we visited my brother and Judy and I witnessed to him; and he accepted the Lord in his life. He later gave us $1200 to move to North Carolina as was indicated in the vision. In 1996, we needed money again to move from one place to another, we just happened to witness to my wife's brother who also gave his life to the Lord, and he also gave us $1600 to relocate to a new residence.

Once the world believes in Jesus, they are no longer "of the world;" but they are now "of" the Lord and His Christ. All we must do is declare that Jesus judged the world by casting out the ruler of the world; knowing that the Holy Spirit is also convicting the world of the same principle; people will be "birthed" to "become … of our

Lord's and His Christ." They will convert to Jesus when they realize that sin or the Devil has no more dominion over them through the cross of Christ. The prince of this world has been cast out of the world. "For **the kingdom** is **the LORD's**, And He rules over the nations" **(Psalm 22:28).**

Satan has no Place (no Authority)!

John 12:31: Now is the judgment of this world; now the ruler of this world will be cast out.

Revelation 12:7-9: [7]And war broke out in heaven: Michael and his angels fought with the dragon; and the dragon and his angels fought, [8]but they did not prevail, nor was a place found for them in heaven any longer. [9]So the great dragon was cast out, that serpent of old, called the Devil and Satan, who deceives the whole world; he was cast to the earth, and his angels were cast out with him.

Ephesians 4:27, KJV: Neither give place to the Devil.

Jesus cast the Devil out of the world! Michael cast the Devil out of heaven! Since these two statements are true, where is the place of the Devil? He has no legal place in the world because Jesus cast him out of the world. Satan has not place in heaven because Michael cast him. The Devil has no place with the saints; because the Bible declared in Ephesians 4:27, KJV, "Neither give place to the Devil." Jesus also declared that **"the prince of this world ... has nothing in me [Jesus]."** Therefore, the Devil has no authority over the saints of the living God; because we are in Jesus, and he is in us.

Note: Satan has a history of "placing" himself among the sons of God. "There was a day when the sons of God came to **present (lit., place)** themselves before the LORD, and Satan came also among them to **present (lit., place) himself** before the LORD **(Job 2:1)**. Therefore, it is not new that Satan likes to place himself among the sons of God, today. Thus, the Father's exhortation saying that we should not "give place to the Devil." This truth is also witnessed in John's vision when he was showed that a "place" was not found for the Devil and his angels in heaven anymore after Michael cast them out of heaven.

With all this truth, the Church must not allow herself to be dominated by any demonic force. We are to judge the world like

Jesus judged the world by casting out devils. We are to judge angels as Jesus did by casting them out of the world into the abyss (Luke 8:28; 31; Revelation 20:3).

1 Corinthians 6:2-3: ²Do you not know that the saints will judge the world? …. ³Do you not know that we shall judge angels? ….

The verses above plainly declared that we would judge the world and angels. Thus, there must be a pattern; and the pattern is given by King Jesus and Michael, the arch angel. Let us look at their example; and then apply their example to our lives.

Satan has **nothing (lit., "not one thing")** in Jesus! Jesus declared, "I will no longer talk much with you, for the ruler of this world is coming, and **he has nothing in Me**" (John 14:30). Jesus "was in all points tempted like as we are, yet **without sin" (Hebrews 4:15)**. 1 John 3:5 declares that "in Him [Jesus] is no sin." Again, Satan has not one thing in Jesus. Thus, Satan has no authority in or over Jesus.

"For this purpose, the Son of God was manifested, that He might destroy the works of the Devil." Here is an application to believers. Colossians 2:10 declares (in the Greek text) that we "are **in Him** having been filled who is **the head** of all principalities and authorities." Those who are filled are considered as being "in" Jesus who is the Head of all principalities and authorities.

It follows that if Satan has not one thing in Jesus, then Satan does not have one thing in us, through our Savior Jesus. We have authority over Satan through Jesus' headship; therefore, Satan has not place in us. Stop letting him and his demons control you! Allow me to recite an even that occurred after my wife taught at a Church.

During the early 2000s, my wife (Judith) went to speak at a Church. After the message, she began to pray for those who desired prayer. There was a sister who came up for prayer. My wife prayed for the lady, freeing her from drugs and any demonic activities. The woman was permanently healed from drugs, immediately (prior to the prayer my wife prayed over the lady that night, the lady has been prayed for numerous times with no permanent result). Judith's account of what happened when she prayed for the lady is interesting. My wife said that she saw Jesus' bodily form walk out of my wife's body, laid hands on the lady, the lady fell to the ground, and then Jesus walked back into my wife's body.

Jesus then said to my wife, remember it is I (Jesus) who is doing the work in you. Again, this lady never went back to abusing drugs; and she is currently doing the work of the ministry completely healed. This is a manifestation of Jesus demonstrating that the prince of this world has nothing in Jesus or any believer.

Jesus has stripped Satan of his strength and Jesus bound Satan! In Matthew 12:29, referencing to Satan, Jesus declared "how can one enter a strong man's [Satan's] house and plunder his goods, unless he first **binds** the strong man? And then he will plunder his house." Jesus **bound** Satan and plunders his house by casting out demons from the bodies of some folks. Luke 11:21-22 also declared that "when a strong man, fully armed, guards his own palace, his goods are in peace. But when a **stronger** than he comes upon him and overcomes him, **he takes from him all his armor** in which he trusted and divides his spoils."

The armor of Satan was his strength. However, the **"stronger [Jesus]** than he [Satan] have come"** upon Satan and took away the armor of Satan's strength. Satan is now bound in weakness because Jesus took Satan's strength. The book of Revelation declared that Satan and his angels were **"not strong enough"** to stand against Michael and his angels. It appears to me that Satan was "not strong enough" to stand against Michael because Jesus already weakened Satan. Here is an application to believers.

Colossians 2:10 declares (in the Greek text) that we "are **in Him** having been filled **who is the head of all** principalities and authorities." Those who are "filled" are considered as being "in" Jesus who is the Head of all principalities and authorities. It follows that since our Head, Jesus, who is also the Head of all angels has showed that He is "stronger" than Satan by stripping Satan of the armor of his strength; then we "in Him" have the same authority over Satan and his angels. **Through the blood of Jesus, we are now stronger than the sin of Satan.** Jesus stripped Satan of his strength; thus, Satan pseudo strength has no place in us. Jesus "did rescue us **out of the authority of the darkness and** did **translate us** into the reign of the Son of His love." **(Colossians 1:13, YLT).**

Jesus cast Satan out of this world; and the saints are to do the same to Satan! [30]"Jesus answered and said, "This voice did not come because of Me, but for your sake. [31]**Now** is the judgment of this world; **now** the ruler of this world will be **cast out"** **(John 12:30-31)**. Satan has no place in the world either. He has been cast out of the world. Paul declared in 1 Corinthians 6:2 that the saints shall judge the world. The logical question is what is Jesus' pattern of judging the world?

Jesus judged the world by casting out the ruler of the world. Thus, the saints are to judge the world by casting out principalities, authorities, powers, controllers, world-rulers, spiritual 'hurts' in heavenly places, and so on. In effect, casting demons out of the world is also the same as judging angels. We are admonished not to give place to the Devil. The same is true for Satan's angels. We are not to give them place. Michael, the arch angel did not give Satan or his angel any place in heaven.

Michael, the arch angel cast Satan out of heaven, because Satan is "not strong enough" to tangle with Michael! [7]"And there was war in heaven. Michael and his angels fought against the dragon, and the dragon and his angels fought back. [8]But he was not **strong enough,** and they lost their place in heaven. [9]The great dragon was hurled down—that ancient serpent called the devil, or Satan, who leads the whole world astray. He was hurled to the earth, and his angels with him." **(Revelation 12:7-9, NIV).**

We learned earlier that Jesus, the "stronger than he (Satan)," stripped Satan of his amour (his strength) **(Luke 11:19-22).** Since Jesus stripped Satan of the armor of his strength, Satan is "not strong enough" any longer. Thus, Michael defeated Satan because the Devils is "not strong enough" to prevail. This was not the first encounter between the Devil and Michael.

After Moses death, the Devil attempted to seize the body of Moses. However, Michael intervened and rebuked Satan through the Lord's authority **(Jude 1:9).** The same is true for all believers today. The Devil has no authority over your body. He also has no place in your heavenly places afforded you in Christ. We now "sit together in **heavenly places** in Christ Jesus" **(Ephesians 2:6).** Yet, our warfare is "against principalities," "against 'authorities,'" "against 'world-strengths'[7] of the darkness of this age" and "against spiritual hosts of wickedness **in the heavenly places" (Ephesians 6:12).** Thus, Michael and his angels also aid us in the heavenly places, like he did for Daniel.

Daniel, the beloved prophet, also encountered some heavenly disturbances from the principality of Persia; and Michael had to come and "bind" the prince of Persia who was attempting to stop another arch angel, Gabriel from imparting to Daniel "what is noted in the Scripture of Truth." The book of Revelation declared that Michael and his angel eventually cast Satan and his angel out of heaven. The results of Michael casting out Satan from heaven were impressive. Salvation came! Power came! The kingdom of God came! The authority of His Christ came! Jesus' blood is magnified! Hear the Scriptures of Revelation 12:7-11, NIV!

> [7]And there was war in heaven. Michael and his angels fought against the dragon, and the dragon and his angels fought back. [8]But he was not strong enough, and they lost their place in heaven. [9]The great dragon was hurled down—that ancient serpent called the devil, or Satan, who leads the whole world astray. He was hurled to the earth, and his angels with him. [10]Then I heard a loud voice in heaven say: "Now have come the salvation and the power and the kingdom of our God, and

---

[7] Greek: kosmokratoras [world (kosmos)-governments (kratoras)]

the authority of his Christ. For the accuser of our brothers, who accuses them before our God day and night, has been hurled down. [11]They overcame him by the blood of the Lamb and by the word of their testimony; they did not love their lives so much as to shrink from death (Revelation 12:7-11, NIV).

Here is an application to believers. Jesus declared that whenever His disciples cast out devils from people, Satan falls from heaven simultaneously. Thus, the authority to cast out demons has a simultaneous affect of also causing Satan to fall from heaven.

Luke 10:17-19, NIV: [17]The seventy-two returned with joy and said, "Lord, even the demons submit to us in your name." [18]He replied, "I saw Satan fall like lightning from heaven. [19]I have given you authority to trample on snakes and scorpions and to overcome all the power of the enemy; nothing will harm you.

When the seventy returned declaring how demons submit to them through Jesus' name, Jesus replied by saying that He saw Satan **"fall"** like lightning from heaven. "Fall" is written in the imperfect tense in the Greek texts. Thus, the verse can read like this: "I saw Satan **'falling'** from heaven."

That is, Satan's "falling" is continuous. Saying it another way, as the Seventy were casting out the demons, there was a simultaneous action in the heavens; Satan is falling from the heaven. Yes, when we cast out demons from people in the earth, simultaneously, Satan is falling from heaven. We have authority to also displace demons from the heavenly places, by the authority Jesus have given us through His Word and His blood.

The blood of Jesus overcomes Satan! [9]"So the great dragon was cast out, that serpent of old, called the Devil and Satan, who deceives the whole world; he was cast to the earth, and his angels were cast out with him. [10]Then I heard a loud voice saying in heaven, now salvation, and strength, and the kingdom of our God, and the power of His Christ have come, for the accuser of our brethren, who accused them before our God day and night, has been cast down. ¹¹**And they overcame him by the blood of the Lamb** and by the word of their testimony, and they did not love their lives to the death" **(Revelation 12:9-11).**

As the Philistines in 1 Samuel 17 could not pass the place called "Ephes Dammin" ("boundary of bloods"), so Satan is overcome by the blood of the Lamb. Satan cannot pass the boundary of the blood of Jesus. The book of Hebrews 12:24 declare that the blood of Jesus "speaks 'stronger' things." Yes, Jesus blood is "better" and "stronger" than any strengths of the enemy. Through His cross, Jesus "disarmed the powers and authorities, he made a public spectacle of them, triumphing over them by the cross" **(Colossians 2:15, NIV).**

Thus, Jesus marginalized Satan; and the Church is to do the same. We should focus on the triumph of Jesus, and the authority of Jesus. In this age, ministers preach more about Satan than they do the All-Powerful God. All of God's ministers need to preach a **mega God** and less and less about Satan pseudo controls. Preachers need to declare the strength of Jesus. If they are going to mention the Devil, declare how weak he is to Jesus and Jesus' blood. Jesus declared in **Matthew 28:18**: "**All authority** has been given to Me in heaven and on earth."

We are to declare the message of Jesus knowing that Satan has no place in the world or in heaven; knowing that Jesus holds all authority, now. The Bible contains about three-quarters of a million words. Satan and his associated names are mentioned significantly less than 0.1% of the time. If God marginalizes the tempter in His Word, so should the Church. Jesus is the head of all principalities and powers, and He "triumphed" over them on the cross. That is, Jesus stripped, disarmed, displaced Satan and all his angels; and Jesus paraded them naked in chains and made a public spectacle of them. Satan no longer has any place or authority in us, in the world or in heaven. The house of Jesus is waxing stronger and stronger (2 Samuel 3:1), and Satan and his angels are waxing weaker and weaker! With that said, here are some examples that demonstrate that Satan has no place among us.

During the early 1990s, we were in Pennsylvania visiting friends and ministering. We were in a home and the lady of the house was concerned that someone she knew was using what the Bile calls "curious arts" or "magic" against her (Acts 8; Acts 19). She asked me to pray, so we prayed and declared that anyone that means her harm cannot come through her doors. That day, a man she knew visited her home (the lady believed that this man was one of the persons using curious arts against her). As the man attempted to enter her home, he was knocked backward, he would try repeatedly and the hand of God or an angel knocked him backward repeatedly as he attempted to enter the home several times and each time he was knocked backward.

Eventually, the man became frustrated and left because no matter how many times he attempted to enter the home, he could not. As we saw this man being prevented by the invisible hand of God to enter the home (apparently, he meant her and us harm), we all stood in awe at the work of the Holy Spirit. This is proof that demons and those satanically motivated can be restricted from having place among us; and we should not give them place.

Recently, my wife (Judith) had an encounter with a lady at a women's meeting. This lady happened to be standing beside my wife and the Lord asked my wife to show the lady love. Soon after my wife had showed the lady love, by hugging her and praying for the lady, the lady began to convulse, contort, and speak in a strange demonic tongue, as the demons (including a python spirit) in this lady manifested.

My wife commanded the demons to go back to the abyss! My wife eventually asked the demons that were manifesting, "Why did you come? Why did you come here?" To which the demons in the woman refused to respond by locking up the woman's body; however, the demon answered the question by the action demonstrated by the woman. The woman began to thrust her pelvic area as if having sexual intercourse. At which point, my wife began to cast out the demons in Jesus name. Judith told one demon after another to come out in the name of Jesus.

In response, the demons attempted to physically take the woman's body with them as they were leaving. The woman started screaming, coughing, throwing up, her head going back and forth in a violent motion, her eyes rolling in the back of her head, legs kicking as each unclean spirit left her. The demons were completely subjected and bound to the name of Jesus. In the encounter with this the woman Judith asked the lady to repent and to accept Jesus as her Savoir.

As indicated in this chapter, Satan and his angels have no place. They have no place in the world because Jesus cast them out of the world. They have not place in heaven, Michael and his angels cast out Satan and his angels. Satan and his angels have no place in the Church. The Holy Spirit by Paul commanded us not to "give place to the Devil."

Satan and his angels must obey the Church when they cast them out of people in the name of Jesus. Satan and his angels cannot renter a person if we command them not to enter no more. Therefore, through the authority of Jesus, we cast out angels, authorities, powers, wicked spirits, etc. from those who are demonized, and these devils have <u>no place</u> in people, in the world, or in heaven.

Mark 9:25-27: 25When Jesus saw that the people came running together, He rebuked the unclean spirit, saying to it, "Deaf and dumb spirit, I command you, come out of him and enter him no more!" 26Then the spirit cried out, convulsed him greatly, and came out of him. And he became as one dead, so that many said, "He is dead." 27But Jesus took him by the hand and lifted him up, and he arose.

Authority over the Elements of the World

Galatians 4:3-7: ³Even so we, when we were children, were in bondage (lit., slavery) under the elements of the world. ⁴But when the fullness of the time had come, God sent forth His Son, born of a woman, born under the law, ⁵to redeem those who were under the law, that we might receive the adoption as sons. ⁶And because you are sons, God has sent forth the Spirit of His Son into your hearts, crying out, "Abba, Father!" ⁷Therefore you are no longer a slave but a son, and if a son, then an heir of God through Christ.

The Bible used the word "element" several times. Element is translated from the word "stoicheion." "Stoichiometry" is derived from "stoicheo;" and it is a word used in chemistry and relates to basic (elementary) substances involved in chemical reactions. "Sstoicheion" means something arranged in a series, to march in ranks, to keep steps. One of its inflections is translated in the New Testament as "walk."

The word "element," in the Scriptures, is used as both positive as it relates to the "walk" of Jesus Christ and "walking" with the Holy Spirit; and negative as it relates to walking in legalism and demon spirits. In addition, through sonship, we have authority over the elements of the world through the Holy Spirit who causes us to walk (element) with Him.

The "elements of the world" appears to be related to walking in step with the world as motivated by spirits borne out in legalism. In the Scriptures, when "element" is used in a negative sense, it was in relation to being taken captive, to slavery, to weakness, to poverty, and being subjected to the dogmatism of legalism. Here are some of the references as it relates to the world.

Colossians 2:8-10, NAU: ⁸See to it that no one takes you captive through philosophy and empty deception, according to the tradition of men, according to the elementary principles of the world, rather than according to Christ. ⁹For in Him all the fullness of Deity dwells in bodily form, [10]and in Him you have been made complete, and He is the head over all rule and authority.

Galatians 4:3, NAU: So, also, we while we were children, were held in bondage under the elemental things of the world.

Galatians 4:9-10, NAU: [9]But now that you have come to know God, or rather to be known by God, how is it that you turn back again to the weak and worthless elemental things, to which you desire to be enslaved all over again? [10]You observe days and months and seasons and years.

Colossians 2:20-22 NAU: [20]If you have died with Christ to the elementary principles of the world, why, as if you were living in the world, do you submit yourself to decrees, such as, [21]"Do not handle, do not taste, do not touch!" [22](which all refer to things destined to perish with use) — in accordance with the commandments and teachings of men?

In Colossians 2:8-10, we are admonished not to walk in step (joined like elements in a chemical reaction) to the world. If we do walk in step with the world, we can be taken "captive through philosophy and empty 'deceptive cheating' according to the tradition of men." Paul then linked this "elementary principles of the world" to spirits called "rule (principality) and authority."

In other words, some of the traditions of men relative to walking in steps with the world are motivated by principalities and powers that will eventually take you captive. That is, a person can become captivated to worldly philosophy — lust of the eyes, lust of the flesh and the pride of provision, worldly holy places — rather than the elementary principles of Christ. A person can become captive to deceptive cheating which leads to emptiness.

In Galatians 4:9-10 and Colossians 2:20-22, "the elemental things of the world" is linked to "bondage" (lit., slavery). These "elemental things" are also called "weak and worthless (lit., poverty)." Thus, if we walk in step with the world, you can be enslaved into observing, days, months, seasons; years; the dogmatic legalism of "do's and don'ts," which will make you enslaved to weakness and poverty.[8] We are not to submit to elementary principles of the world that dogmatically say, "Do not handle, do not taste, do not touch!" According to Romans 14, it is weak to observer certain days, weak to only eat vegetable, and weak to ban certain drinks because of dogmatism.

Some may read the paragraph above and say what is the big deal about the dogmatism of legalism? God has rules! God has laws! God does indeed have rules that are **"spiritual"**! Dogmatism in wrong application is important because it was dogmatism (judgments according to appearance[9]) like this that led to some crucifying the Lord Jesus. For example, the Pharisees "observed days." They so observed the Sabbath that they sought to destroy Jesus for healing on the Sabbath.

Mark 3:1-6, NAU: [1]He entered again into a synagogue; and a man was there whose hand was withered. [2]They were watching Him to see if He would heal him on the Sabbath, so that they might accuse Him. [3]He said to the man with the withered hand, "Get up and come forward!" [4]And He said to them, "Is it lawful to do good or to do harm on the Sabbath, to save a life or to kill?" But they kept silent. [5]After looking around at them with anger, grieved at their hardness of heart, He said to the man, "Stretch out your hand." And he stretched it out, and his hand was restored. [6]The Pharisees went out and immediately began conspiring with the Herodians against Him, as to how they might destroy Him.

The elementary principle of legalistic dogmatism (in this case "observing days") can be taken so far that it caused people to kill Jesus; and it will cause people to also kill Christians. There was a man with a withered hand in the synagogue, while Jesus was there in the synagogue. However, "they were 'observing' Him to see if He would heal him on the Sabbath." Therefore, the Pharisees were "observing days" — the Sabbath day. Jesus became angry at them and asked is it lawful to do well or do harm on the Sabbath. Of

---

[8] Compare Jeremiah 5:4
[9] John 7:23-24

course, they kept silent. In addition, Jesus proceeded to exercise authority over their elementary principle of observing a day by healing the man on the Sabbath.

In our days, the elementary principle of dogmatic legalism prevails in most Churches. There are some in slavery to observing the Sabbath day; and they do this in the name of Christ. However, if you study Jesus' life, He exercised authority over the Sabbath. In fact, Jesus said, **"The Sabbath was made for man, and not man for the Sabbath" (Mark 2:27).** The Father made the days for you. He did not make you for the days. You are lords of the days! How can I make this statement? Jesus said the same thing! Jesus said, "The Son of Man is also Lord of the Sabbath" **(Luke 6:5)**

There are some who are enslaved to "months" (new moons, new seasons). They are in slavery to observing a new season, a new phase for most of what they do. These people move in phases (governed by the power of the "lunar" rather than the authority of the Father). They have their lunar (monthly) revivals! Some observe months by looking too deep into the zodiac observations; months also points to the some in the Church being enslaved to worldly seasonal events (i.e., Easter, Valentine, and so on).

There are also some who observe years! Every New Year there is a prophetic word for that year. I am not so sure God spoke to all those people who say that every year God changes the word for the last year and give another word for the New Year. The god of New Year is a two-faced god. On face looks back, the other face looks forward; and this god is worshipped very year by the world and some Christians. There are yearly pastors' anniversaries, yearly Church anniversaries; there are choir day, men's day, women's day, youth day, fund raising day, Valentine's day, Father's Day, mothers' day! Is your head spinning yet for all these observing of days, months, and years? Please read the Bible and study how Jesus lived! Jesus was not controlled by years, days, and months!

Another other area of the elementary principle of the world is the area of dogmatism as it relates to "not handling" certain things, "not tasting" certain things and "not touching" certain things. Some people think it is a sin to "handle" certain things; for example, there are some who are afraid to be touched by sinners! Who touched you to heal you? There are some who are afraid to touch Jesus! Jesus is touchable. "He can be **touched** with the feelings of your weaknesses" **(Hebrew 4:15).** This word touch also relates to sexuality. Thus, some are afraid to "touch" their spouses in an intimate manner because of religious dogmatisms. The last time I checked God created sex and said the sex organs are not defiling (Hebrews 13:4)!

The dogmatism of legalism is also at work through those who are condemning saints or people who "taste" what some so-called preachers deems as wrong, i.e., drinking wine, eating pork, etc.[10] Paul said, "Let no man therefore judge you in meat or in drink." The Bile said, "every creature of God is good, and nothing to be refused, if it be received with thanksgiving: For it is sanctified by the word of God and prayer" (see **1 Timothy 4:1-5).** The Bible said drunkenness is forbidden, not drinking. The disciples drank real wine for communion in the days of Jesus, in the days of the apostles of the lamb and in the days of the apostle Paul. The problem was that some in the Church at Corinth abused drinking. They abused drinking by getting drunk with the communion wine.

1 Corinthians 11:20-22: [20]Therefore when you come together in one place, it is not to eat the Lord's Supper. [21]For in eating, each one takes his own supper ahead of others; and one is hungry, and another is drunk. [22]What! Do you not have houses to eat and drink in? Or do you despise the church of God and shame those who have nothing? What shall I say to you? Shall I praise you in this? I do not praise you.

In the verses above, it is obvious that fermented wine was been used for communion, as seen in Paul's statement: "one is hungry,

---

[10] 1 Tim 3:8; Matt 11:19, 1 Tim 4:4-5

and another is **drunk**." The problem was, some of the disciples were eating up the communion bread and food before the rest of the saints arrived; and they were also getting drunk with the communion wine. Paul then declared that if they wanted to stuff themselves with food and get drunk, they should do it in their homes. Why? They have not "discerned the Lord's body."

That is, they have not discerned that the bread and the wine is a symbol of Jesus' body and blood; and they should not be used "in an unworthy manner" by glutton and drunkenness. "For he who eats and drinks in an unworthy manner eats and drinks judgment to himself, not discerning the Lord's body" **(1 Corinthians 11:29).** Just as God killed Aaron's two sons, Nadab and Abihu, for offering "strange fire" — offering **incense** (a symbol of prayer) while they were drunk; Paul stated that if any saint gets drunk at the Lord's Supper with the communion wine, it will bring judgment to the abusers.

Leviticus 10:1-2; 8-11: ¹Then Nadab and Abihu, the sons of Aaron, each took his censer and put fire in it, put incense on it, and offered profane fire before the LORD, which He had not commanded them. ²So fire went out from the LORD and devoured them, and they died before the LORD.... ⁸Then the LORD spoke to Aaron, saying: ⁹"Do not drink wine or intoxicating drink, you, nor your sons with you, when you go into the tabernacle of meeting, lest you die. It shall be a statute forever throughout your generations, ¹⁰"that you may distinguish between holy and unholy, and between unclean and clean, ¹¹"and that you may teach the children of Israel all the statutes which the LORD has spoken to them by the hand of Moses."

1 Corinthians 11:26-27; 33-34: ²⁶For as often as you eat this bread and drink this cup, you proclaim the Lord's death till He comes. ²⁷Therefore whoever eats this bread or drinks this cup of the Lord in an unworthy manner will be guilty of the body and blood of the Lord.... ³³Therefore, my brethren when you come together to eat, wait for one another. ³⁴But if anyone is hungry, let him eat at home, lest you come together for judgment. And the rest I will set in order when I come.

Thus, no one (preachers or chief people in the Church) should be drunk or drinking while they are ministering in "meetings" (Leviticus 10:9); and/or while they are ministering in the **"inner court"**[11] (Ezekiel 44:21). "Inner" in the Hebrew text is plural and is from a root word that means "faces." Thus, there should be no drinking for leader or saints when they are ministering in the "face" (presence) of God in prayer, study, fasting, worship, teaching, prophesying, Church meetings, etc.; or in the "faces" of people (saved or unsaved) during holy meetings, evangelisms, praying for the sick, and so on.

In 1 Timothy 3:2, Bishops (overseers) are commanded to be "<u>not</u> given to wine." Some have used this verse as a legalistic tool to forbid drinking. However, here are some of the literal definitions of the Greek word used for "given to wine." "Given to wine" literally means, "one who sits sit long at his wine" (Thayer); "addicted to wine" (Friberg), "quarrelsome over wine," "brawler," "abusive" (Thayer); "drunkard" (Louw-Nida; Strong's). This word used in Timothy and Titus is geared more towards a warning about abusing drinking. Jesus said He came "eating and drinking" and they called Him a **"winebibber,"** or "drunkard" **(Matthew 11:19).** For those who are legalistic about drinking, how do you handle Jesus' statement that even Jesus Himself drank fermented wine?

With that said, a person should also not prophesy "for" wine and "for" strong drink.[12] Understand also that wine can "batter" a person.[13] Believers must also be very considerate of those whose "consciences" are "weak" towards certain days, foods, and drinks.[14] However, we must not condemn people to hell for

---

[11] Note: This word "court" is from a root word that means to surround with a trumpet sound. This is linked to the seven angels with the seven trumpets in Revelation 8 and relates to the prophetic. You may reference my books The Days of the 7th Angel and Ezekiel-the House-the City-the Land (Interpreting the Patterns)

[12] See the Hebrew text and and/or the Septuagint (LXX) for Micah 2:11

[13] Isaiah 28:1, "overcome" (KJV) is also defined as "battered."

[14] 1 Corinthians 10:29-33 w/Romans 14:6; 14:21-22

drinking.[15] There are some who refuse to "handle" certain things! They feel that they are not allowed to handle the things of God, due to the condemnation of humanistic doctrine. The slavery to the elements of **"handle not"** will make it seem like the things of God are off limits. These people see themselves and others as not clean enough to do the works of God.

Yet, we all were unclean before we met Jesus. "But you were **washed,** but you were **sanctified**, but you were **justified in the name of the Lord Jesus** and **by the Spirit** of our **God" (1 Corinthians 6:11).** Jesus said to the disciples, after His ascension,[16] "Behold My hands and My feet, that it is I Myself. **Handle Me** and see, for a spirit does not have flesh and bones as you see I have" **(Luke 24:39).** Handle Jesus! There is a real and living flesh and bone Jesus who can now be handled by us. We have been made clean by Jesus and His Holy Spirit.

Thus, we now have authority over the elements of the world that attempts to enslave us. Times—days, months, years—and the dogmatism of "do's and don'ts" do not govern us. We received this authority when we became sons of God through Jesus Christ and the Holy Spirit. However, we must walk responsibly (1 Corinthians 6:12; Galatians 5:13).

Galatians 4:1-5: [1]Now I say that the heir, as long as (lit., as long as uninterrupted time) he is a child, does not differ at all from a slave, though he is master of all, [2]but is under guardians and stewards until the time appointed (lit., preplaced) by the father. [3] Even so we, when we were children, were in bondage (lit., slavery) under the elements of the world. [4]But when the fullness of the time (lit., the filling of the uninterrupted time) had come, God sent forth His Son, born of a woman, born under the law, [5]to redeem those who were under the law, that we might receive the adoption as sons (lit., the placing as sons).

---

[15] 1 Timothy 5:23; 1 Corinthians 11:21-22; Romans 14:14 w/14: 17 w/14:20-21; Psalm 104:14-15
[16] John 20:17

In the verses above, we see that a "child" can be "master (lord) of all;" yet that "child" is no different from a slave … until **the filling of uninterrupted time** preplaced by the Father. Thus, uninterrupted time is linked to immaturity. In addition, Galatians 4:4 said when the "filling of interrupted time had come, God sent forth His Son." Thus, the Son, Jesus, interrupted time when the Father placed Him. A mature son interrupts time. An immature son is controlled by the cycle of time as dictated by the elements of the world.

Jesus was placed as the mature Son in the "filling of 'chronos' (time)." Jesus was under "guardians and stewards until the 'uninterrupted time.'" But when Jesus was "placed" ("This is My Beloved Son, in whom I am well pleased.") as the Son of God at His baptism in water, Jesus was no longer under "guardians and stewards."

This means that all the "elements of the world" is subjected to Jesus. Jesus, as the mature Son, dominated the elements of the world. Jesus the mature Son interrupted time in the filling of time. Jesus did not let the Sabbath, or His day of death deter Him for God's purposes. The same is true for the other sons of God (us). Jesus brothers (us) will be placed as sons, by the mature Son, Jesus. In Galatians 4, we learned that time was interrupted by Jesus, the Son of God. Paul also stated that we were also children, "in 'slavery' under the elements of the world. But when the fullness of the time had come, God sent forth His Son … that we might receive the adoption as sons (lit., the placing as sons)."

We as "placed" mature sons now dominate the elements of the world, which includes "times" — days, months, years, religious dogmatism, etc. Remember, the seventh angel or the seventh trumpet declared that "the kingdoms of this **world** became of our Lords and of His Christ" **(Revelation 11:15).** The elements of the world also are subjected to His Christ.

The mature sons are no longer "in 'slavery' under the elements of the **world**" **(Galatians 4:3).** As indicated earlier, "elements of the world" are linked to "days" (a form of time), "months" (a form of time), "seasons" (a form of time), and "years" (a form of time). Jesus, as the mature "placed" Son conquered the elements of the world. Jesus interrupted time. Jesus interrupted the cycle of death. Time is death. God said to Adam, "In the **day** that you eat of it you shall **surely die**" **(Genesis 2:17).**

Thus, time ("in the day") is linked to "dying by death." Jesus destroyed the time of death. Jesus laid down His life when He wanted to; and Jesus picked up His life in three days by the authority of the Father **(John 10:17).** No one could take Jesus' life at their will **(John 10:18).** The elements of the world are made subject to God's sons!

Yes, time and death are made subject to the Father's mature Son — Jesus and His other mature sons (those in the Church of Jesus who attain to maturity). Yes, dogmatisms of "do's and don'ts" are no longer the standard. Outward dress and rituals are not the standards. Authority is not in a robe! Authority is not in long public prayer! Authority is not in religious rituals (outward ceremonies)! Authority is not in a dolly that covers the head of a woman!

Authority over the elements of the world is found in the Son of God — Jesus. "Therefore, you are no longer a slave but a son, and if a son, then an heir of God through Christ" **(Galatians 4:7).** Since you are a son of God, you are "lord of all" the elements of the world **(Galatians 4:1). What this 'lordship" means is that "all" must do what you say!**

Luke 6:46: But why do you call Me 'Lord, Lord,' and do not do the things which I say?

Galatians 4:1, KJV: Now I say, that the heir, as long as he is a child, differs nothing from a servant, though he be lord of all.

Galatians 4:6-7: 6And because you are sons, God has sent forth the Spirit of His Son into your hearts, crying out, "Abba, Father!" 7Therefore you are no longer a slave but a son, and if a son, then an heir of God through Christ.

Once we become "sons" (lit., mature sons), we become "Lord of all." We are no longer "a slave" or "a child," or "non-speaking. We do not need "permitters" or stewards over us. We are now maturing enough to speak to every situation as Jesus also spoke and saw immediate results.

We are now "lords," "similar" to our Lord Jesus Christ. Revelation 19:16 states that Jesus is the "Lord of lords;" and we are the "lords" that He is Lord of! Jesus also states that if He is indeed our Lord, and Jesus is our Lord, then we would do the things which He says (see Luke 6:46-49). It follows that since we are now sons of God, which means we are "lord of all," then all the elements of the world must also "do what we say." We have authority as sons to be "lord of all." "All" the elements of the world (spiritual and physical) must now obey us and do what we say.

Here are examples our authority as sons. In the early 1990s one summer while living in North Carolina, a sister came to me with her daughter. Her daughter's hair was patchy from her hair falling out and noticeably short. When I saw them, I felt deep compassion for them. The mother asked me to pray for her daughter, showing me how hair daughter's hair was falling out. The little girl was sad about her hair. I laid my hands on her hair and head and prayed.

About thirty (30) days later, the lady returned with her daughter showing me and Judith the result of the prayer. The Lord caused the young girl's hair ("her glory") to re-grow all the way down to the middle of her back. Note: this was a Black girl, and her hair had grown down to the middle of her back without any "perm" in her hair. When, they came by I could not grasp how quickly her hair had grown back, not just an inch or two; but her hair had grown down to the middle of her back. They were so happy and appreciative for what the Lord had supernaturally done for them. This is a manifestation of God's authority over the element that was attached to the young girl's hair.

My wife and I were living in Owings Mills, Maryland. At the time, I was a carpenter. We were making just enough money to pay the lease, gas and electric, etc. Two of our five children were born at the time. We needed some food and asked a sister (Margie Epps) for some help. She gave us $20. We went to the store to buy what we could with the $20. When, we got home and began to bring in the grocery, we realized that there were a lot more bags on the table than $20 could by.

The bags of grocery multiplied before our eyes; and for some reason, moisture appeared on the bags; and for some reason the sight of the sprinkled water on the grocery bags stood out and was very refreshing to look at. Things that we needed appeared in bags as we unpacked the grocery bags, rejoicing in the Lord. As proven by Jesus in the Scriptures when He multiplied the fish and the loves, Jesus is still showing that He is the Lord over all the elements of the earth, including food and provisions.

Around the early 1990s, we lived in a trailer in North Carolina. At that time in our lives, there were times when we did not have enough money to provide heating for the trailer. One night, it became very cold. For some reason that night, I felt really empowered to speak to the elements, as I could feel the cold of the night enter the trailer; boldness came over me; and I spoke to the cold and said, "Cold you will not enter this trailer tonight!" The cold stopped outside the trailer, literally; and we were warm that night. As I looked out of the door of the trailer, I could see the cold like a mist form around the trailer, but the cold did not and could not enter the trailer. Even, the climate conditions must obey us. Jesus exemplified this with the wind and the sea.

Matthew 8:23-27: 23Now when He got into a boat, His disciples followed Him. 24And suddenly a great tempest arose on the sea, so that the boat was covered with the waves. But He was asleep. 25Then His disciples came to Him and awoke Him, saying, "Lord, save us! We are perishing!" 26But He said to them, "Why are you fearful, O you of little faith?" Then He arose and rebuked the winds and the sea, and there was a great calm. 27So the men marveled, saying, "Who can this be, that even the winds and the sea obey Him?"

Mark 1:27: Then they were all amazed, so that they questioned among themselves, saying, "What is this? What new doctrine is this? For with authority, He commands even the unclean spirits, and they obey Him."

Luke 10:17-20: [17]Then the seventy returned with joy, saying, "Lord, even the demons are subject to us in Your name." [18]And He said to them, "I saw Satan fall like lightning from heaven. [19]"Behold, I give you the authority to trample on serpents and scorpions, and over all the power of the enemy, and nothing shall by any means hurt you. [20]"Nevertheless do not rejoice in this, that the spirits are subject to you, but rather rejoice because your names are written in heaven."

Jesus' Holds Every Authority

Matthew 28:18, NIV: Then Jesus came to them and said, "All authority in heaven and on earth has been given to me."

All (lit., every) authority has been given to Jesus! Every authority that exist in heaven or on earth, Jesus exercise supreme authority over them. Jesus holds all authority in heaven and on earth. Therefore, every heavenly being is under Jesus' authority, every earthly being is under Jesus' authority; and every being under the earth is under Jesus' authority. Jesus is He "who has gone into heaven and is at the right hand of God, angels and **authorities** and powers having been made **subject** to Him" **(1 Peter 3:22).** With that said, hear a list of some of the evil authorities identified in the Bible that Jesus is now Lord over them.

1. Authority of Satan **(Acts 26:18)**

2. Authority of darkness **(Luke 22:53)**

3. Authority of the air **(Ephesians 2:2)**

4. Authority of the world **(Luke 4:5-6)**

5. Authority of Herod **(Luke 23:7)**

6. Authority of death and hell **(Hebrews 2:14; Revelation 6:8)**

7. Authority of the beast **(Revelation 13:2; 4-5; 7; 12)**

8. Authority of the ten kings **(Revelation 17:12)**

Here is some of the authority that Jesus exercised in the Bible.

1. The authority to teach **(Mark 7:29)**

2. The authority to heal by only a word **(Matthew 8:8-9)**

3. The authority to forgive sins **(Matthew 9:6)**

4. The authority against unclean spirits **(Matthew 10:1)**

5. All authority in heaven and earth **(Matthew 28:18)**

6. The authority to command unclean spirits **(Mark 1:27)**

7. The authority to give authority to His disciples **(Mark 6:7)**

8. The authority to give authority to His servants **(Mark 13:34)**

9. His words were in authority **(Luke 4:32)**

10. The authority to cure all diseases **(Luke 9:1)**

11. The authority over serpents and scorpions **(Luke 10:19)**

12. The authority over all the powers of the enemy **(Luke 10:19)**

13. The authority to kill and cast into Gehenna **(Luke 12:5)**

14. The authority to give authority over cities **(Luke 19:17)**

15. The authority to give authority to become children of God **(John 1:12)**

16. The authority to execute judgment **(John 5:27)**

17. The authority to lay down His life and to resume His life **(John 10: 18)**

18. The authority over all flesh to give them life **(John 17:2)**

19. The authority of the Father to restore the kingdom to Israel **(Acts 1:6-7)**

20. The authority of God **(Acts 26:18)**

21. The authority to make a vessel unto honor or dishonor **(Romans 9:21)**

22. The supreme authority **(Romans 13:1)**

23. The authority over angels and authorities **(1 Peter 3:22)**

24. The authority over death and hell **(Revelation 1:18; 6:8)**

25. The authority to give authority over the nations **(Revelations 2:26)**

26. The authority over locust from the abyss **(Revelation 9:4)**

27. The authority to give the authority of the two witnesses **(Revelation 11:6)**

28. The authority of His Christ **(Revelation 12:10)**

29. The authority over the fire of the Altar of Incense **(Revelation 14:18)**

30. The authority over plagues **(Revelation 16:9)**

31. The great authority **(Revelation 18:1)**

32. The authority over the second death **(Revelation 20:6)**

33. The authority to the tree of life **(Revelation 22:14)**

With the above "authority" of our Lord Jesus outlined, allow me to share an even that also happened through the Holy Spirit a few years ago. There are some in the earth who do not really understand that Jesus holds "every" authority. The Father, His Son, Jesus, and the Holy Spirit have authority to even kill the body; and the Father, the Son and the Holy Spirit have authority to cast that body into Gehenna—a place of burning **(Luke 12:4-5).** In the earth "priest" may appear to "rule by their own means" (Jeremiah 5:31). They really do not "fear" God. However, Jesus our "Chief Priest"[17] and our "'Great' Priest"[18] "do" exercise all authority in the kingdom of men.

Here is what the Lord God said through Moses, "Now see that I, even I, am He, and there is no God besides Me; I kill, and I make alive; I wound, and I heal; Nor is there any who can deliver from

---

[17] Hebrews 8:1
[18] Hebrews 10:21

My hand" **(Deuteronomy 32:39)**. Here is a prophetic word the Lord gave me in 2002, which demonstrate the "all authority" of Jesus.

On April 25, 2002, the Lord woke me up early that morning. I got on my knees to pray and saw Jimmy Swaggart[19] and I also heard his name. I saw what he had accomplished as an evangelist. I then saw what he had become after his exposure which was related to impure sexuality and his repetition of these acts that he was accused of, and how he has become a byword in the land among some saved and some unsaved. I then began to pray for him that he would be restored. (I thought that was the reason the Lord brought him to my attention in the vision I was seeing) However, as I prayed, the Holy Spirit stopped me in the middle of my prayer; and my ears dilated and the Holy Spirit said, "Others, who have done like he has done, will also be exposed."

I then heard Him say "He (the Holy Spirit) will be removing priests from the earth" (Acts 5; Ezekiel 9). My presumptuous prayer for him ended. I continue to listen as I saw the Pope and I sensed that God was about to remove him by death also; as I continued to look, I saw what appeared to be Eli. Then the scripture was heard in my ears "I will do things in your day that will cause the ears of people to tingle" — again, during this encounter my ears were literally being dilated to hear (I could feel and see the dilation). It appears that Eli represented the Pope who like Eli did not correct his sons who were priests; therefore, God allowed Eli (a type of the Pope) to die, and God killed Eli's sons (priests)?

Within **two weeks** I heard on the news how a Catholic priest was shot being related to inappropriate sexuality. Another hanged himself. Months later, another priest got killed in prison. Ironically, Pope John Paul II, died three years later in the same month (April)

---

[19] Please note that I did not place the name here to put down anyone. The Lord would sometimes name names of some through His prophets in the Bible (Ezekiel 8:11; 11:13; Isaiah 28:15-17; 1 Timothy 1:18-20)

the Lord showed me this vision. The Holy Spirit spoke this prophetic word to me independent of any news and prior to its fulfillment. The prophet Amos said in **Amos 3:7,** "Surely the Lord GOD does nothing, unless He reveals His secret to His servants the prophets." The Lord, who created us, exercises "all authority" in heaven and on earth. God who created us can also remove us from the earth if He so authorizes it.

A few years back, a false prophet came to our Church at one of the seminars we held. This prophet began to have "diarrhea of the mouth," and he was attacking me, and he was putting down the work the Lord gave us to complete. He also attempted to assault me physically, which prompted some of the brothers in our Church to stand up to protect me.

I stood up that Sunday and indicated to the Church that God did not send that prophet and that he had to be careful because of what he spoke against our ministry. I also explicitly said that this prophet had to be careful what he said because the Lord would remove him from the earth for saying "God says" if God did not speak to him to "say." Within a year or so that prophet died (compare Jeremiah 28 when a false prophet died within seven months after prophesying lies to God's people and compare Ezekiel 11:13). I was later told that this man, who calls himself a prophet, was not submitted to any authority and was a busy body. "[13]Let us hear the conclusion of the whole matter: **Fear God and keep His commandments,** for this is man's all. [14]For God will bring every work into judgment, including every secret thing, whether good or evil" **(Ecclesiastes 12:13-14)**.

Authority in the "Now!"

John 12:31: Now is the judgment of this world; now the ruler of this world will be cast out.

Revelation 12:10, NIV: Now have come the salvation and the power and the kingdom of our God, and the authority of his Christ

Hebrews 11:1: Now faith is the substance of things hoped for, the evidence of things not seen.

2 Corinthians 6:2: For He says: "In an acceptable time I have heard you, and in the day of salvation I have helped you. Behold, now is the accepted time; behold, now is the day of salvation."

1 John 3:2a: Beloved, now we are children of God ….

We are to live in the "now." However, some are more conditioned to live in the "if" realm and the "tomorrow" realm that we scarcely walk in the authority of His Christ, "now." In the mind of some, everything is always tomorrow. Some live in the realm of "ifs." We often hear the questions of the "what if God is not in it?" These are some of the thieves ("if" and "tomorrow") in the lives of some. Dr. Kelley Varner taught us that there were two thieves on their respective crosses when Jesus was crucified. One (1) thief was the thief of the past which I call the thief of doubt; the other thief was the thief of putting everything in the future. However, Jesus in the middle of them lived in the "today."

One thief was Satan personified in the flesh. He gave himself away when he used the same "if" statement of doubt that he used against Jesus in Jesus' original forty days of temptation. The thief (Satan personified in the flesh) said, "If You are the Christ save Yourself and us." Satan used this same "if" phrase in the wilderness temptation of Jesus. "The devil said to Him, **'If You are the Son of God**, command this stone to become bread'" **(Luke 4:3).** "Then he brought Him to Jerusalem, set Him on the pinnacle of the temple, and said to Him, **'If You are the Son of God,** throw Yourself down from here'" **(Luke 4:9).** Thus, we have to understand that whenever God tells us to do something and we get bombarded by the "if" (doubt) factor, then doubt is linked to the thief Satan. With that said, the other thief is defined as the "future."

"Then he said to Jesus, 'Lord, remember me **when** You come into Your kingdom. And Jesus said to him, 'Assuredly, I say to you, **today** you will be with Me in Paradise.'" **(Luke 23:42-43).** This thief points to our tendencies to put most of what we think God has for us to future time. "Remember me when You come into your kingdom." However, Jesus countered this thief of the future by saying, whatever the Father has for us can happen "today;" as it is written, "[Jesus] say to you, **today** you will be with [Him] in Paradise."

We must live in the **"now"** realm that Jesus lived in and is still living in. Jesus declared that "now is the judgment of this world." Not tomorrow, but **now.** This means that Revelation 11:15 is true **now!** The authority of His Christ is now! "The kingdoms of this world have become the kingdoms of our Lord and His Christ." Yes, "now" are the kingdoms of the world become of our Lord and His Christ! This is true because Jesus judged the world. Jesus cast out he ruler of the world approximately 2,000 years ago. Jesus declared that "now the ruler of the world will be cast out."

Jesus made this "now" declaration about His death by crucifixion. The same cross that Satan used to crucify Jesus is the same cross the Father used to cast Satan out of the world. This was exemplified by an enemy of the Jew Mordecai called Haman. The same "gallows" (lit., tree) that Haman erected to hang Mordecai, is the same "gallows (lit., tree) that the king used to hang Haman **(Esther 7:9-10)**. Paul also exemplified this truth in 1 Corinthians 2. Paul declared that if the rulers of this age had known the glory that would be distributed by Jesus to His saints after His crucifixion; they would not have crucified Jesus. That is the crucifixion of Jesus has defeated the ruler and bringing "to nothing" the rulers of this age.

> [6]However, we speak wisdom among those who are mature, yet not the wisdom of this age, nor of the rulers of this age, who are coming to nothing. [7]But we speak the wisdom of God in a mystery, the hidden wisdom which God ordained before the ages for our glory, [8]which none of the rulers of this age knew; for had they known, they would not have crucified the Lord of glory (1 Corinthians 2:6-8).

Thus, Jesus **"now"** rules over the kingdom of the world forever and ever. Jesus cast out Satan approximately 2,000 years ago. The cross of Christ is bringing the rulers of this age and rulers of this world to nothing. The ruler of the world is "now" cast out of the world. Jesus is Ruler of all, now! Jesus is not the soon coming King! He is King now because **Jesus was born King!**

In Matthew 2:2, when the Magi who came from the east sought out Jesus in His youth, they shocked Herod and Jerusalem when they asked, "Where is He who has been **born King of the Jews?"** Jesus is the King of the Jews, now! Jesus is the King of the nations, now! Jesus is the King of the world, now! Jesus is the King of His Church, now! Jesus was "born King."

We also must live in the "now" relative to the salvation, the power, the kingdom of God and the authority of His Christ. This is realized when we understand that Michael cast Satan out of heaven. This is realized when we cast out demons from the world and out of people. **"Now** have come the salvation and the power and the kingdom of our God, and the **authority of his Christ"** **(Revelation 12:10, NIV)**.

If we lack power let us pray until Michael and his angels dislodge any demons that is affecting our sphere of the heavenly realm. If we are not seeing "the salvation," let understand that "now is come the salvation." "Now is the day of salvation." Let us seize the opportunity to save some, by walking in the "now." If "the kingdom of God" is not come in our lives and the lives of others, let us allow the Holy Spirit to manifest the Kingdom of God in us, now—righteousness, peace, and joy in the Holy Spirit **(Romans 14:17).**

Michael ejected Satan and **"now** has come … the kingdom of God and the authority of His Christ." The "now faith" transcends time and space. There is "delay no longer" as declared by the angel in Revelation 10:6. **"Now** [has] come … the authority of His Christ!' "Behold, **now** is the accepted time; behold, **now** is the day of salvation." "Beloved, **now** we are children of God."

Allow me to cite some examples. In 1987, after returning to America from a one-year tour of duty in Okinawa, Japan (I was in the USMC at the time); I was stationed in North Carolina. The car my wife and I owned needed new brakes; and it also had electrical issues that affected the rear lights. My first day reporting for duty, I was told by the MP (Military Police) that after that day, I could no longer drive the car on the Base until I had those issues fixed (the brakes were so bad, they could be heard, and the lights were flickering). At that time Judy and I were married for a year; and my military pay was just enough to get by.

Thus, we had no way of fixing the car; and we needed the car to be fixed **"now."** How was I to show up for duty without a car? We were new to the area and the Base, and we knew no one. So, we prayed and asked God so send his angel to fix the car. The Father answered our prayer. God sent his angel and fixed the brakes and the lights. This may not be important to some? However, because we had no money to fix the car, we knew no one in the area; it meant so much to us that God sent His angel to fix the car for us **immediately.**

Another time, around 1988, I accompanied a pastor to visit a woman in a crazy home. She asked us to pray. The pastor and I laid our hands on the lady and prayed. As I prayed, I **immediately** and **physically** felt virtue (ability of God's power) leaving my hand and going into this woman like a stream of water from a hose. When we got finished praying, the lady turned to me and said, "When you prayed for me, I felt virtue leave you, and enter my body."

About two (2) weeks later she was released from the crazy home; and she came to Church. Again, this is a manifestation of the "now" realm of God, as He wills it to happen.

While ministering prophetically to some saints in North Carolina during the early 1990s, I approached to a couple to pray for them. I asked them what they wanted from the Lord. The husband indicated to me that the wanted children. However, they could not have children because his sperm count was exceptionally low per a doctor's analysis. The Holy Spirit in me began to prophesy (declare) to them that they would have children. It was not long after that (a couple of years later) I heard that they had at least two children without any medical aid. The Lord remembered them and gave them children.

During the early 2000s, my wife and I were invited to preach in Pennsylvania at Apostle Earl Palmer. On this day Judith was finishing her session by praying for the ladies. (Pastor Palmer and I returned to the sanctuary where the ladies were meeting after he and I finished speaking to the men.) As we sat in the back of the seating area, and as Judith continued praying, I witnessed a lady sitting around the last row where the ladies were gathered. I could see that she had been subjected to a walking cane with bandages on her foot. As Judith continued to pray, the Holy Spirit healed the woman on the spot, **immediately.** She leaped up and began to jump around saying "I am healed," "I am healed" as she began to thank God, running and holding other sisters telling them what had just happened to her. She was so elated about her supernatural healing; she kept going around to the many saints saying that she was healed. Again, this is a manifestation of the "now" realm of God.

Let us reject the thief of tomorrow. We can be healed today, not just tomorrow. We can raise the dead today, as Jesus wills it. We can cleanse the lepers today. We can cast out demons, now. The Father can move on our behalf now, as He chooses. The father can judge the world "now," if he chooses. Let us reject the thief of doubt. The thief that says, "If you are a child of God, then, why is this, and why is that?" Let us, accept the teaching of our Lord Jesus, "now." We are under Jesus' authority now! Thus, we can use his authority now! "Now [has] come … the authority of His Christ"

Authority — the New Doctrine!

Mark 1:27: Then they were all amazed, so that they questioned among themselves, saying, "What is this? What new doctrine is this? For with (lit., in) authority He commands even the unclean spirits, and they obey Him."

Jesus came in the flesh and introduced a "new doctrine." He introduced the doctrine of casting out demons "in authority." "They were all amazed …saying …what **new doctrine** is this? For **'in' authority** He commands even the unclean spirits, and they obey Him." Prior to Jesus demons were dealt with by exorcist that used oaths; however, Jesus changed that by operating in the authority of the Son of God.

Acts 19:13-18: [13]Then some of the itinerant Jewish exorcists took it upon themselves to call the name of the Lord Jesus over those who had evil spirits, saying, "We exorcise you by the Jesus whom Paul preaches." [14]Also there were seven sons of Sceva, a Jewish chief priest, who did so. [15]And the evil spirit answered and said, "Jesus I know, and Paul I know; but who are you?" [16]Then the man in whom the evil spirit was leaped on them, overpowered them, and prevailed against them, so that they fled out of that house naked and wounded. [17]This became known both to all Jews and Greeks dwelling in Ephesus; and fear fell on them all, and the name of the Lord Jesus was magnified. [18]And many who had believed came confessing and telling their deeds.

"Exorcist" as used in the reference above literally means "one that binds by oath (or spell)" (see Strong's Concordance). Straight from the Greek compounds, it means "to oath-out of" ("ek" — out of and "horkos" — oath). Thus, one can easily see that demons were exorcised "out of" people by "oaths," among the Jews. One can also see how powerless and un-authoritative the exorcists were (seven exorcists were "traumatized" by one demon). However, Jesus changed this and merely used the authority of His words to cast out demons. Unlike the exorcists, demons had to obey Jesus and come out of people, unconditionally.

Mark 1:27: Then they were all amazed, so that they questioned among themselves, saying, "What is this? What new doctrine is this? For with (lit., in) authority He commands even the unclean spirits, and they obey Him."

Luke 4:35-36: 35But Jesus rebuked him, saying, "Be quiet, and come out of him!" And when the demon had thrown him in their midst, it came out of him and did not hurt him. 36Then they were all amazed and spoke among themselves, saying, "What a word this is! For with authority and power He commands the unclean spirits, and they come out."

In Luke's account of the people's reaction when Jesus cast out the demon, Luke replaced the word "doctrine" used by Mark with the word, "word." Mark's account states that the people said, "What **new doctrine** is this? For 'in' authority He commands" Luke's account state that the people said, "What a **word** is this? For 'in' authority and power He commands" Thus, the **"new doctrine"** of Jesus is to casts out demons in the authority of His **"word."**

Jesus does not have to use an oath as the unauthorized exorcist of that day and some of today use. The Father authorizes Jesus to cast out demons with His word. You also as sons of God have been authorized to cast out demons by your word. We have been authorized to use the name of Jesus to cast out demons. This is part of the doctrine of Jesus' authority!

Matthew 10:1, NIV: He called his twelve disciples to him and gave them authority to drive out evil spirits and to heal every disease and sickness.

Mark 6:7: Calling the Twelve to him, he sent them out two by two and gave them authority over evil spirits.

Luke 10:17-19: 17Then the seventy returned with joy, saying, "Lord, even the demons are subject to us in Your name." 18And He said to them, "I saw Satan fall like lightning from heaven. 19"Behold, I give you the authority to trample on serpents and scorpions, and over all the power of the enemy, and nothing shall by any means hurt you."

Mark 16:17: And these signs will follow those who believe: In My name, they will cast out demons; they will speak with new tongues.

Acts 16:16-18: [16]Now it happened, as we went to prayer, that a certain slave girl possessed with a spirit of divination met us, who brought her masters much profit by fortune-telling. [17]This girl followed Paul and us, and cried out, saying, "These men are the servants of the Most High God, who proclaim to us the way of salvation." [18]And this she did for many days. But Paul, greatly annoyed, turned, and said to the spirit, "I command you in the name of Jesus Christ to come out of her." And he came out that very hour.

There is a new doctrine introduced by Jesus. Demons can be cast out "in the authority" of the "name of Jesus Christ." This "new doctrine" of casting out demons through the "words" of the name of Jesus is to be used by His disciples "today." Yet there are so many who are afraid to cast out demons. I have discovered through the Scriptures that if someone is afraid to cast out demons, this fear is linked to "superstition."

Acts 17:22-23, KJV: [22]Then Paul stood in the midst of Mars' hill, and said, Ye men of Athens, I perceive that in all things ye are too superstitious. [23]For as I passed by, and beheld your devotions, I found an altar with this inscription, TO THE UNKNOWN GOD. Whom, therefore, you ignorantly worship, him declare I unto you.

The word "superstitious," used in the reference above, is a compound of two words which literally means to "dread-demons." "Dread" is defined as reluctance to do, extreme apprehension, reluctance to face an apparent overwhelming circumstance. In Acts 17:22-23, their fear of demons (superstition) caused them to erect an altar to their superstition. The same is true today. Some people are so fearful of demons, they erect altars to them. That is, they do all kind of ridiculous rituals to appease their superstitious beliefs. I have been in Churches where preachers open physical doors to let the demons out once they claim they cast out the demons. They were afraid that the demons would repossess someone else. This is a ridiculous superstition.

Jesus was **not** superstitious. Jesus commanded the demons by His words what to do and what not to do. "When Jesus saw that the people came running together, He rebuked the foul spirit, **saying** unto him, you, dumb and deaf spirit, **I charge thee**, come out of him, and **enter no more** into him" **(Mark 9:25, KJV).** Jesus used the authority of His words to restrict demons from reentry. Jesus charged the demons "come out of him and enter no more." He was not afraid of demons. He did not pacify them. Jesus was not superstitious. On the contrary, they were afraid of Him.

Luke 8:28-29a, KJV: [28]"When he saw Jesus, he cried out, and fell down before him, and with a loud voice said, what have I to do with thee, Jesus, thou Son of God most high? I beseech thee, torment me not. [29](For he had commanded the unclean spirit to come out of the man ....)."

Jesus established a new doctrine. He cast out unclean demons "in authority" and with His "words." Jesus authorized His disciples to do the same. We can cast out demons through words saying, "Come out in the name of Jesus." We are not to be fearful of demons by superstitions. All demons and elemental spirits must submit to us through the name of Jesus. Here are some of my experiences.

Around 1989, while living in Owings Mills, Maryland, we were having Bible study at the home of a sister in Christ named Margie Epps. A man came to the study whom Judy (my wife) and I were acquainted with when we were younger. I saw that demons were plaguing him. I asked him to stop by my house the next day for me to pray for him. To my surprise, he did come by the following night around 10:00pm. I prayed for him by casting out the demons in the name of Jesus Christ until 3:00am in the morning.

Three hundred (300) demons came out of him. As I prayed for him and cast the demons out of him by words in the name of Jesus, the demons would call out their names; and each time a demon came out, the lights in our house would blink. I must also note that as I was casting the demons out of this man, his eyes would roll in his head, and all that could be seen was the white of his eyes. Also, his head was moving back and forth so fast, it seems like his head was spinning.

Finally, when I attempted to cast out the last demon, he refused to go and would attempt to drag the body of the man out of the building. The first three hundred left, but this last one who called himself Satan, did not appear to have left (I was a young minister then and did not fully understand my authority in Christ with regards to this last demon that was so stubborn to leave). The next day, I asked our pastor to pray for the man to complete the process.

During the year 1992, I was in Pennsylvania visiting friends and ministering. One night after I taught on "the coming of the Lord," the congregation began to pray. This gentleman kept inquiring about the teaching. He asked would the coming of the Lord happen as I taught. As he kept pacing, he repeated the question. He kept asking me was the word that I taught true? I said yes, the Word is true! Apparently, the Word that was taught was bringing deliverance to the young man.

As we continued to pray to the Father and praying in the Spirit this same man began to scream with a loud, deep beastly voice, I then saw a muscular-like demon that looked like the swamp thing, with its extra-long arms dragging the ground came out of a man and walked out the back door of the house. The man was delivered that day without any human laying hands on him. The "finger of God" and the Word of God was at work to cast this demon out.

In 2011 a young man came to me requesting prayer. He relayed to me how he was losing his mind and how something was taking over his body. He was so demonically influenced that he was jailed for losing his mind and going out into the street naked. After I listened to his story, I laid my hand on him and prayed for him by casting out the demon in the name of Jesus Christ. He became stiff as a board and fell to the sofa as the spirit left him. After he came to himself, he said that he was shivering and felt very cold (I gave him a shirt to warm himself); he also could not look at the light of the day for a few moments (apparently the spirit that was oppressing him had cover his spiritual eyes and natural with literal darkness).

In 2010 while in Jamaica West Indies preaching, a lady stood up at one of the meetings and stated that after she heard the message, I had taught the night before, while she was at home, she felt this violent shaking and a significant tug in her lower back. Apparently, she had back pain issues; however, the pain was not from a physical damage. A spirit of infirmity caused the back problems. She continued by saying that she felt a pull and a shaking as the spirit and the pain left her body. She declared that night that she was healed from the back pains and credited it to the words she was hearing through the messages.

These examples were provided to show you that Jesus' doctrine of casting out demons in His name is still functioning today. Jesus authorizes us to cast out demons through His name! And the demons must obey us! As the seventy said to Jesus, "Lord, even the demons are subject to us in Your name."

Jesus brought a "new doctrine" in the earth. This new doctrine is relevant today. We have been given the authority to cast out demons by using words, saying, "in the name of Jesus Christ come out of that person;" just as our Master Jesus also did when he walked the earth in flesh and blood.

With that said, let us also realized that there are levels of the effectiveness of casting out demons. What I mean is that some demons will exit immediately upon the spoken word. Yet some demons may take an hour to leave, depending on the type of demons. While some "species" of demons only come by prayer and fasting. This is good to know so as not to give up so easily on people when results are not as immediate as one would expect. Here are three examples of what I just indicated.

1. **Immediate** deliverance. That is, at Jesus' word demons came out "immediately."

Luke 13:10-13: ¹⁰Now He was teaching in one of the synagogues on the Sabbath. ¹¹And behold, there was a woman who had a spirit of infirmity eighteen years and was bent over and could in no way raise herself up. ¹²But when Jesus saw her, He called her to Him and said to her, "Woman, you are loosed from your infirmity." ¹³And He laid His hands on her, and immediately she was made straight, and glorified God.

Jesus healed the woman "immediately" from a "spirit of infirmity" that Jesus named "Satan," in verse sixteen (Luke 13:16).

2. Deliverance in an **"hour."** That is, it took Paul about an hour to cast out a python spirit.

Acts 16:16-18: ¹⁶Now it happened, as we went to prayer, that a certain slave girl possessed with a spirit of divination met us, who brought her masters much profit by fortune-telling. ¹⁷This girl followed Paul and us, and cried out, saying, "These men are the servants of the Most High God, who proclaim to us the way of salvation." ¹⁸And this she did for many days. But Paul, greatly annoyed, turned, and said to the spirit, "I command you in the name of Jesus Christ to come out of her." And he came out that very hour.

3. Some demon species came out by a lifestyle of **"prayer and fasting."**

Matthew 17:15-16; 18-21: ¹⁵"Lord, have mercy on my son, for he is an epileptic and suffers severely; for he often falls into the fire and often into the water. ¹⁶"So I brought him to Your disciples, but they could not cure him." ¹⁸And Jesus rebuked the demon, and it came out of him; and the child was cured from that very hour. ¹⁹Then the disciples came to Jesus privately and said, "Why could we not cast it out?" ²⁰So Jesus said to them … ²¹"However, this kind does not go out except by prayer and fasting."

The Greek texts for the phrase "This kind does not go out except by prayer and fasting," literally reads: "this **'species'** does not go out except **'in'** prayer and fasting." This is important to understand. Jesus' disciple must be constant "in prayer" and must be constant "in fasting" to cast out certain "species" of demons. That is, the Father so empowered Jesus "in prayer" and "in fasting" that stubborn "lunatic" (or "epileptic") demons and stubborn "deaf and dumb spirits" were cast out "immediately" and "in that very hour."

Mark 9:17-18; 23-29, KJV: [17] And one of the multitude answered and said, Master, I have brought unto thee my son, which hath a dumb spirit; [18] … and I spoke to thy disciples that they should cast him out; and they could not …. [23] Jesus said unto him, if thou can believe, all things are possible to him that believeth …. [25] … Jesus … rebuked the foul spirit, saying unto him, thou dumb and deaf spirit, I charge thee, come out of him, and enter no more into him. [26] And the spirit … came out of him: and he was as one dead … [27] But Jesus took him by the hand and lifted him up; and he arose. [28] And when he was come into the house, his disciples asked him privately, why could not we cast him out? [29] And he said unto them, this kind can come forth by nothing, but by prayer and fasting.

Authority of the Two Witnesses

Revelation 11:6, YLT: These have authority to shut the heaven, that it may not rain rain[20] in the days of their prophecy, and authority they have over the waters to turn them to blood, and to smite the land with every plague, as often as they may will.

Revelation 16:9, YLT: And men were scorched with great heat, and they did speak evil of the name of God, who hath authority over these plagues, and they did not reform—to give to Him glory.

There is an authority (the authority to plague) that will surely stir debate. However, as a prophet of the Lord, I must state His purposes which include authorization to His Church to smite with plague as God directs. This authority is exercised not arrogantly, but mournfully "clothed in sackcloth" (Revelation 11:3). The two witnesses in Revelation which consists of Jesus' Church, the olive trees and the two prophets, were authorized to plague the land. Why was this authorization given? God desires people to repent and give Him glory! Yes, the purpose of God sometimes plaguing the earth is to bring people to repentance. Before I discuss His authority to plague the earth, let us look at what result God was expecting, but did not necessarily get it from the people.

Revelation 16:9, NIV: They were seared by the intense heat, and they cursed the name of God, who had control over these plagues, but they refused to repent and glorify him.

Revelation 16:11, NIV: And cursed the God of heaven because of their pains and their sores, but they refused to repent of what they had done.

Revelation 9:20-21, NIV: [20]The rest of mankind that were not killed by these plagues still did not repent of the work of their hands; they did not stop worshiping demons, and idols of gold, silver, bronze, stone, and

---

[20] Greek: shower

wood—idols that cannot see or hear or walk. ²¹Nor did they repent of their murders, their magic arts, their sexual immorality, or their thefts.

Revelation 2:21-22: ²¹I have given her time to repent of her immorality, but she is unwilling. ²²So I will cast her on a bed of suffering, and I will make those who commit adultery with her suffer intensely, unless they repent of her ways.

These references in the book of Revelation I just listed gave me comfort. These verses showed me the heart of God in the middle of all of His judgments. He disciplined because He wants all of us to "repent" (lit., "change [our] mind") of any evil **practices.** Thus, one of the purposes of His authorization to plague the earth is to bring humanity to repentance. In Revelation 2:18-29, we learn of a false prophetess who were committing adultery, fornication, idolatry, and teaching others to do the same. God "gave her time to repent."

However, He eventually judged her because she was "unwilling" to "repent" (change her mind). God does not take pleasure in the death of the wicked. "He is patient with you, not wanting anyone to perish, but everyone to come to repentance" **(2 Peter 3:9).**

In Revelation 9:13-20, we also learn that God plagued the earth with beasts of horses with horsemen. These beasts had lions' heads, horses' bodies, and tails with serpents' heads. "Their 'authority' is in their mouth and in their tails." "Fire" (including "fever"), smoke (judgments related to sexual sins) and brimstone (place of lightning) came out of their mouths.

One third (1/3) of mankind was killed by these plagues. "But the rest of mankind, who were not killed by these plagues, **did not repent** .... And they did **not repent** …" **(Revelation 9:20).** Here we see the purpose of the plague of the sixth trumpet. God's goal is to bring mankind to repentance—a changing of their minds "that they should **not** worship demons, idols of gold, silver, brass, stone, and wood, which neither can see nor hear nor walk. And they did

not repent of their murders or sorceries (lit., drugging) or their sexual immorality or their thefts" **(Revelation 9:20-21).**

In Revelation 16:8-11, we learned again that the purpose of the plague of the scorching sun, plague of darkness on the kingdom of the beast (government that rule the world), and the plague of pain in them was to bring them to repentance. Instead "they cursed the name of God who had 'authority' over these plagues … they refused to **repent** and glorify Him" **(Revelation 16:9, NIV).** "They refused to **repen**t of what they had done" **(Revelation 16:11, NIV).** Allow me to recite to you an event.

Around 1996, at Sunday morning service, as we were praying for the people, I felt the hand of the Lord on me strongly with regards to a couple that attended the Church, especially the husband. I indicated to him by the Spirit that he is to be faithful to his wife and not to commit adultery against her because God had called them to be pastors. The Lord also said to him (the husband) that if he did not heed the voice of the lord to serve the Lord that Satan would attempt to kill him (compare 1 Timothy 1:20; 1 Corinthians 5:4-5). It was later reported to me that evening by the pastor of the Church that the man left Church that day and went out to buy crack cocaine; and he was shot in the chest.

However, the Lord had mercy on him and allowed him to live. I was also told that the bullet could not be removed from his body. The next Sunday the entire Church building was filled through the fear of God. Apparently, the people spread the word to the surrounded community, and many started to attend Church again.

In addition, the next time I saw that man, he had apparently lost his luxury car, he was dressed in rags and was using the mass transit system. He spoke to me with a little smile and went about his way. Apparently, he did not repent to heed the Lord's instruction, and thus he appeared to have lost all his substance.

With that said, God "has **control (lit., authority)** over … plagues;" and He has given this authority to be executed in the earth through

His two witnesses. The two witnesses are made up of "the two lampstands (or candlesticks);" "the two olive trees;" and the "two prophets."

Revelation 11:3-4; 10: ³" And I will give power to my two witnesses, and they will prophesy one thousand two hundred and sixty days, clothed in sackcloth." ⁴These are the two olive trees and the two lampstands standing before the God of the earth.... ¹⁰And those who dwell on the earth will rejoice over them, make merry, and send gifts to one another, because these two prophets tormented those who dwell on the earth.

The first of the two witnesses are the two olive trees. The second of the two witnesses are the two lampstands. The third of the two witnesses are two prophets. These two witnesses were given "authority" to stop rain, "authority over water to turn them to blood," and "'authority' ... to strike the earth with all plagues as often as they desire" **(Revelation 11:5-6).** Yet who are these two witnesses; and how do they relate to Jesus' Church?

First, let us establish that "two" (2) is a number that represents "witness;" as it is written, "in the mouth of **two** or **three witnesses** every word may be established" **(Matthew 18:16, KJV).** The meaning of the two witnesses of the two olive trees is this: Paul in Romans 11:11-24 taught that the "olive tree" is made up of both Jews and Gentiles.

Thus, through the Church age, and during the seasons of the last hour of this age and the first hour of the new millennium,²¹ the two witnesses of the olive trees (Jewish believers and Gentiles believer) stand up in the earth with authority to preach "the testimony" (Jesus); and they will torment the nations by releasing plagues in the earth to bring the rest of humanity to repentance (Revelation 11:9-10).

---

²¹ For more information on the last hour, the first hour, please refer to my books The Last Hour, The First Hour, The Forty-second Generation

The two olive trees are also a symbol of the witness of the "sons of oil." These are the sons of God who have been filled with oil from the bowl of God's fountain with the "golden oil" of the Holy Spirit (Zechariah 4:3; 14). These are the sons of God who supply the oil of the Holy Spirit they received from the fountain of God to the "candlesticks" the Churches of Jesus Christ (Philippians 1:19; Zechariah 4:11-12).

In Zechariah 4, we see a picture of a candlestick. Above this candlestick was a "bowl" from which "gold oil" flowed to the two olive trees also beside the candlestick. The word "bowl" in the Hebrew also means "fountain." Thus, this bowl was the "fountain" that supplied the "golden oil" to the candlestick for the candlestick to produce light. The oil is the source of the light of the candlestick. We learn in Zechariah 4:3-12 that the oil flows from the fountain of the bowl, into the two olive trees, then through the two olive trees, into the candlestick with its seven lamps.

The same is true for the two witnesses of the two lampstands or candlesticks in Revelation 11. The two olive trees supply the oil (the Holy Spirit) to the two candlesticks. The book of Revelation 1:20 state that the candlestick is symbolic of the Church. Thus, the two olive trees (the sons of oil) were empowering the witness of the Churches (the candlesticks) to show the Light of Jesus. Demonstrating Jesus (the light of the candlesticks) is the witness.

The Church must be supplied with the Holy Spirit for her light (the works of God she does) to shine as a witness. "But you will receive power when the Holy Spirit comes on you; and you will be my witnesses in Jerusalem, and in all Judea and Samaria, and to the ends of the earth" **(Acts 1:8).** It is clear, we also need the "Holy Spirit … to be [Jesus'] witnesses." This truth bears out in Revelation 11; the two candlesticks need the oil of the Spirit to be supplied by the two olive trees in order "to be [Jesus'] witnesses … to the ends of the earth."

The two witnesses of Revelation 11 were also called "two prophets" (Revelation 11: 10). Before, I speak to this; let us look at the definitions of the two witnesses. The two witnesses are called "two olive trees" (a symbol of the Church made up of Jews and Gentiles); the two witnesses are also the two olive trees which are also a symbol of the "sons of oil" (the Fathers' sons who have matured to be like Jesus); and the two witnesses are also the two lampstands (candlesticks), which we also saw that they are symbolic of the Church of Jesus.

Now if you can receive what I am about to say, it follows that the two witnesses of the two prophets are also symbolic of the witness of prophets in the Church and also symbolic of the body of Christ that will operate as prophets in the earth. This concept of corporate body being called prophets is not new. The Lord called Israel His "anointed ones and His **"prophets"** (1 Chronicles 16:13-22).

The Churches of Jesus have been authorized to be witnesses in the earth before Jesus' ascension in Acts 1:8 and are continued to be authorized as His witnesses in the earth as demonstrated in Revelation 11:1-13. The Church (the corporate body of Christ) has been authorized to "finish 'the' testimony" — "the testimony of Jesus" (Revelation 11:7; 19:10).

The Church (the corporate body of Christ) has been authorized to flow in the same authority Moses and Elijah demonstrated. Moses turned the water of Egypt into blood (Exodus 7:17-21). The two witnesses have authority to do the same according to Revelation 11:6. Elijah caused it not to rain for 3 ½ years in Israel (1 Kings 17:1-2; James 6:17-18). The two witnesses were given the same authority according to Revelation 11:6.

Here is the mind that has wisdom. Malachi prophesied that Elijah would come before Jesus; Malachi also said to remember the Law of Moses (Malachi 4:5-6). Some of the Jews believed that Elijah would come in person (Matthew 17:10-13). Jesus said that Elijah came in the form of John, the Baptist (Matthew 11:12-14). Moses was a prophet like unto Jesus (Acts 7:37).

Jesus was not Moses; Moses was not Jesus. The same is true for the two witnesses; some believe that Moses and Elijah will come again. The two witnesses are not Moses and Elijah. On the contrary, the two witnesses of the Church will flow **as** two prophets in the same authority and power of Moses and Elijah.

The two witnesses of the Church of Jesus are His two olive trees, His two lampstands and His two prophets! Yes, (using a little bit of humor here) I know that God's math is "fuzzy." That is, you would think that 1+1=2; however, in God's math 2 olive trees + 2 candlesticks=2 witnesses; or 2 olive trees + two candlesticks + 2 prophets=2 witnesses. The Church of Jesus Christ has the authority to be His two witnesses!

I conclude this chapter on the two witnesses, with a revelation the Lord gave me concerning the sixth trumpet in Revelation 9. This is the trumpet that caused one-third of mankind to be killed; and yet, they refused to repent. If you can receive what I am about to say, receive it; if you cannot receive it, may the Lord give you understanding and wisdom.

Around 1993, I frequented the Lord, seeking understanding from the book of Revelation. One night I mediated all night on Revelation 9: 13-20 repeatedly the entire night. As I mediated deep into the morning hours, I saw a great light radiating from the Bible I was reading (meditating in). The light remained until the morning.

At around 7:00am the Holy Spirit opened the scriptures of Revelation 9:13-20 to me. Light and revelation flooded the spirit of my mind. The revelation was so overwhelming and rich, that morning I wanted to teach what the Lord revealed to me. However, the Lord told me that I should not teach it at that time.

When I did go to Church that morning, one of the elders said to me that my countenance was very shiny. I knew then that the great light I saw coming from the Bible was also imparted to my face as well. That morning the Spirit of the Lords revealed to me that the four angels were **"internally prepared"** to kill one-third of humanity, thus they had to be bound. In other words, because they there were prepared internally to kill, they had to be kept bound until the time of their release.

Once they are released, the four angels became (multiplied to) two hundred million horses and horsemen. They killed with fire (including "fever"), smoke (which includes judgment in the blood of them that practice same sexuality), and brimstone (lightning strikes against humanity). The "great river Euphrates" is symbolic of these horsemen "gushing forth" upon the one-third of mankind. The four angels were being "loosed" from being four (4) angels to multiply, themselves, into 200,000,000[22] horsemen.

These angels can be released for "an hour, a day, a month, a year" as God sees fit. The sixth bowl in which the great river Euphrates is dried up is a symbol of the plagues of the 200,000,000 horses and horsemen being dried up. The Lord later showed me that the voice from the four horns of the golden altar that authorized the sixth angel to trumpet includes the voice of the blood of Jesus. The golden altar of incense was anointed with the blood of the sacrifice once a year (Leviticus 16:17-19).

So likewise, the blood of Jesus has been sprinkled on all the heavenly vessels (Hebrews 9). Jesus' blood speaks (Hebrew 12:24). Thus, the voice from the four horns of the golden altar includes the voice of the blood of Jesus. Jesus authorized through intercession (symbolized by the golden altar), the voice of His blood to release the judgment of the sixth angel with the sixth trumpet. That is, there is the mercy of Jesus through His blood even in the judgment of the sixth seal (Hebrews 12:24).

"6This is He who came by water and **blood—Jesus Christ,** not only by water, but by water and **blood**. And it is the Spirit who bears witness because the Spirit is truth. 7For there are three that bear

---

[22] Some ancient Greek manuscripts indicate 100,000,000

witness … ⁸ … the Spirit, the water, and the **blood**; and these three agree as one. ⁹If we receive the witness of men; the witness of God is greater; for this is the witness of God which He has testified of His Son. ¹⁰He who believes in the Son of God has the witness in himself; he who does not believe God has made Him a liar, because he has not believed the testimony that God has given of His Son. ¹¹And this is the testimony: that God has given us eternal life, and this life is in His Son. ¹²He who has the Son has life; he who does not have the Son of God does not have life" **(1 John 5:6-12).**

Who gave you this Authority?

First, we must understand that there is no authority, but God's. No one is "in" authority, except the Father, Jesus, and the Holy Spirit. Anyone, except for the Father, Jesus and the Holy Spirit who say that they are "in" authority, watch out! Understand that for anyone to exercise authority, he/she must be "**under** authority." Anyone who is not "under" the authority (God) is a usurper! Authority is given and can only be exercised from within! You can easily tell when a person has no authority; power (ability) cannot be demonstrated! People can recognize those who are under authority and those who have no authority!

Luke 20:1-8: [1]Now it happened on one of those days, as He taught the people in the temple and preached the gospel, that the chief priests and the scribes, together with the elders, confronted Him [2]and spoke to Him, saying, "Tell us, by what authority are You doing these things? Or who is he who gave You this authority?" [3]But He answered and said to them, "I also will ask you one thing, and answer Me: [4]"The baptism of John—was it from heaven or from men?" [5]And they reasoned among themselves, saying, "If we say, 'From heaven,' He will say, 'Why then did you not believe him?' [6]"But if we say, 'From men,' all the people will stone us, for they are persuaded that John was a prophet." [7]So they answered that they did not know where it was from. [8]And Jesus said to them, "Neither will I tell you by what authority I do these things."

Jesus walked in so much authority that men began to question Him concerning the source of His authority. Jesus' teaching and preaching was so effective that the chief priest, the scribes, the elders "confronted" Jesus saying. "Tell us, by what authority are You doing these things? Or who is he who gave You this authority?"

Something similar happened to me many, many years ago. I taught a message the Lord gave me from the book of Genesis, Chapters 1-3. I taught on the order of creation relative to Adam, the beasts of the field,[23] Mrs. Adam and the **ground** from which they were formed. After, I finished the teaching; the leader of the ministry came to me and asked me in a very derogatory manner, "Where did you get such revelation from?" In other words, where did I get the authority from to teach such things? The minister also indicated that I would not be preaching again for at least six months. I submitted to his wishes.

Men have tried to intimidate me; however, the Lord has said to me "be white (pure) and fear no man." With respect to Jesus being questioned, Jesus was assertive in His response; especially since Jesus perceived their insincerity, He left them without any absolute answer, yet Jesus did give them the answer. Jesus answered their question within His counter question.

"But He answered and said to them, I also will ask you one thing, and answer Me: The baptism **of John** — was it **from heaven** or **from men" (Luke 20:4)**? Jesus answered their question, within His counter question. Jesus' authority was from heaven and from man (John, the Baptist). Yes, God the Father gave Jesus His authority from Heaven; and John, the Baptist, authorized Jesus when he baptized Jesus in the Jordan River. In other words, John testified that Jesus is the Son of God and the Father testified that Jesus is His Son. Jesus was authorized both by the testimony of the Father of heaven and the testimony of a man, John the Baptist.

> [29]The next day John saw Jesus coming toward him, and said, "Behold! The Lamb of God who takes away the sin of the world! [30]"This is He of whom I said, 'After me comes a Man who is preferred before me, for He was before me.' [31]"I did not know Him; but that He should be revealed to Israel, therefore I came baptizing with water." [32]And John bore witness, saying, "I saw the Spirit descending from heaven like a dove, and He remained upon Him.

---

[23] Note: "The beasts of the field," or living creatures of the spread (Genesis, chapters 2 and 3) were created after "the beasts of the earth" (mute beasts like cattle) (Genesis 1); refer to my book When the Lord Made the Serpent

³³"I did not know Him, but He who sent me to baptize with water said to me, 'Upon whom you see the Spirit descending, and remaining on Him, this is He who baptizes with the Holy Spirit.' ³⁴"And I have seen and testified that this is the Son of God" (John 1:29-34).

²¹When all the people were baptized, it came to pass that Jesus also was baptized; and while He prayed, the heaven was opened. ²²And the Holy Spirit descended in bodily form like a dove upon Him, and a voice came from heaven which said, "You are My Beloved Son; in You I am well pleased" (Luke 3:21-22).

The Father gave Jesus His authority when the Father declared Jesus to be His Beloved Son. John, the Baptist, also authorized Jesus when John baptized Jesus. John declared: "I did not know Him, but He who sent me to baptize with water said to me, 'Upon whom you see the Spirit descending, and remaining on Him, this is He who baptizes with the Holy Spirit.' And I have seen and testified that this is the Son of God."

Now note: If our King Jesus, our Savior Jesus, our Lord Jesus had to be authorized by the Father and a man (John, the Baptist in order "to fulfill all righteousness"), why do so many of today disregard the authority of God, and only follow the personal dictates of men ("men pleasers"); and why do some disregard the authority of Jesus' five-fold ministries (men and women) and claim that they do not need to be under the authority of humans?

Jesus was not a man pleaser. Yet, Jesus submitted to the authority of man to fulfill all righteousness. In fact, The Father authorized Jesus as His Mature Son, after Jesus commanded John, the Baptist to fulfill all righteousness by Baptizing Jesus.

Matthew 3:15-17: ¹⁵But Jesus answered and said to him, "Permit it to be so now, for thus it is fitting for us to fulfill all righteousness." Then he allowed Him. ¹⁶When He had been baptized, Jesus came up immediately from the water; and behold, the heavens were opened to Him, and He saw the Spirit of God descending like a dove and alighting upon

Him. [17] And suddenly a voice came from heaven, saying, "This is My Beloved Son, in whom I am well pleased."

Jesus submitted to the authority of John (a man); even though Jesus Himself said that He does not need the testimony of man. The father's testimony was adequate for Jesus. However, God has so ordained that man must also authorize man. Some human being must also testify of our (your) authority for us to flow **"under"** authority! Yet, in the same token, do not let overbearing so called men of God control you to the point of "men pleasing."

John 5:32-37: [32] "There is another who bears witness of Me, and I know that the witness which He witnesses of Me is true. [33] "You have sent to John, and he has borne witness to the truth. [34] "Yet I do not receive testimony from man, but I say these things that you may be saved. [35] "He was the burning and shining lamp, and you were willing for a time to rejoice in his light. [36] "But I have a greater witness than John's; for the works which the Father has given Me to finish—the very works that I do—bear witness of Me, that the Father has sent Me. [37] "And the Father Himself, who sent Me, has testified of Me. You have neither heard His voice at any time, nor seen His form.

There you have it again, the testimony (authorization) of man is not as important as the authorization of the Father. However, the testimony (authorization) of man is needed. Jesus cited John, the Baptist, and the Father as the witness of His authority as the Son of God. Jesus referenced "heaven" (the Father's Throne) and John in Luke 20 when His authority was questioned; and Jesus again cited John and the Father as His witness that Jesus is indeed authorized to be "in authority!"

With that said, when Jesus came on the scene about 2,000 years ago, one of the things that stood out was Jesus authority. The people noted that Jesus was not like the Scribes and Pharisees. They took note that Jesus walked in authority!

> [21] Then they went into Capernaum, and immediately on the Sabbath He entered the synagogue and taught. [22] And they were

astonished at His teaching, for He taught them as one having authority, and not as the scribes. ²³Now there was a man in their synagogue with an unclean spirit. And he cried out, ²⁴saying, "Let us alone! What have we to do with You, Jesus of Nazareth? Did You come to destroy us? I know who You are— the Holy One of God!" ²⁵But Jesus rebuked him, saying, "Be quiet, and come out of him!" ²⁶And when the unclean spirit had convulsed him and cried out with a loud voice, he came out of him. ²⁷Then they were all amazed, so that they questioned among themselves, saying, "What is this? What new doctrine is this? For with (lit., in) authority He commands even the unclean spirits, and they obey Him." (Mark 1:21-27)

I get excited about our Lord every time I read the Scriptures above. Jesus was not like the Scribes. The Scribes teaching were without authority. This is understood to mean in modern time, the Scribes teaching were boring; because they had no authenticity to substantiate their teaching. On the contrary, Jesus backed up His teaching by demonstration "in authority."

The doctrine of Lord is also **"what"** the Lord does! "**And they were astonished at His teaching, for He taught them as one having authority, and not as the scribes ...** they were all amazed, so that they questioned among themselves, saying, "What is this? What new doctrine is this? **For with (lit., in) authority He commands even the unclean spirits, and they obey Him**" (Mark 1:21; 27).

Jesus was authoritative! Jesus is the authority! Jesus walked "in authority." There is no authority unless it is **"under God."** This was Jesus' strength. He was under God's authority in order to flow in authority! As indicated at the beginning of this Chapter, to exercise authority, you must be under God's authority.

Romans 13:1: Let every soul be subject to the governing authorities. For there is no authority except from (lit., under) God, and the authorities that exist are appointed by (lit., under) God.

In the verse above "governing authorities," literally reads in the Greek texts as: "hold-above authorities," or "high-above authorities," or "supreme authorities." The phrase "For there are no authority except from God," literally reads in the Greek texts as: **"there is no authority, if not under God."** The rest of the verse that reads: "and the authorities that exist are appointed by God," literally reads; "and the [authorities] that exist are arranged **under God**."

This is particularly important to know. **There is no authority, if [the authority] is not under God."** The scribes had no authority because there were not planted by the Father; that is, they were not "under" God's authority (Mark 1:22; Matthew 15:13). The Centurion, who asked Jesus to heal his bondservant, understood this kind of authority that flows from submission to the "supreme authority" — God, the Father. The Centurion understood that Jesus authority is only working, because Jesus was <u>under</u> the authority of God.

Matthew 8:5-10: [5]Now when Jesus had entered Capernaum, a centurion came to Him, pleading with Him, [6]saying, "Lord, my servant is lying at home paralyzed, dreadfully tormented." [7]And Jesus said to him, "I will come and heal him." [8]The centurion answered and said, "Lord, I am not worthy that You should come under my roof. But only speak a word, and my servant will be healed. [9]"For I also am a man under authority, having soldiers under me. And I say to this one, 'Go,' and he goes; and to another, 'Come,' and he comes; and to my servant, 'Do this,' and he does it." [10]When Jesus heard it, He marveled, and said to those who followed, "Assuredly, I say to you, I have not found such great faith, not even in Israel!"

Hear the language of the Centurion. He said that he was "**also** … **under authority** … and I say to this one, 'Go,' and he goes; and to another, 'Come,' and he comes …." The Centurion could exercise authority because he was **"also** … under authority." He fully understood this same truth concerning Jesus. He knew that Jesus was under the authority (totally submitted to the Father); and thus, Jesus could exercise authority upon others by speaking "a word." This was God's principle used by the Roman government, unknowingly. The Romans expected submission to authority, which in turn, allowed authority to flow. The Centurion understood this order being a Roman soldier.

Jesus was totally submitted to the "supreme authority" of the Father; and thus, He flowed "in (the) authority" of God. The same is true for all saints, we must submit to the authority of Jesus (and He was given "every authority"), in order to flow under His authority. There are so many self-appointed apostles, prophets, evangelists, pastors, teachers, and so on, who are not under the authority of the Father; and **"there is no authority, if [the authority] is not under God."** With that said, we must also understand that authority is from within and should also be self-evident. That is, authority should be authentic (self-authoritative).

A collector's item is **authentic** because it is apparently self-authoritative.[24] The Greek word for "authentic"[25] is a compound of two words: "auto" (self) and "hentes" (domineering). Thus, something is authentic when it is self-authoritative. The item's "self" is so "domineering," it is self-evident. That is, authority may only flow out of a people who know who they are in Christ. He or she understands that they are made in the image of God. They understand that "they exist" out of God. They have an authentic identity within their self that is defined by God.

"Authority" is from the Greek word "exousia." "Exousia" is a compound of two words, "ek" (out of) and "eimi" (I exist, I am). Thus, authority is apparent when we understand that "we exist out of" God. There is **no** authority if the authority is not under God. We must know that our "existence" is "out of" God in order for us to walk in submission under God, the Father. Our "identity" (our "I exist") is linked His authority.

---

[24] A statement made by Dr. Myles Monroe
[25] Note: the word "authentic" as used in 1 Timothy 2:12 originally meant one who kills himself/herself with his/her own hands. It later came to also mean "self-authoritative," domineering, etc.

Authority flows out of the "I AM" into our "self" who "exists" in the image of God. Through, Jesus you must understand that "I am" ("you exist" out of God) because I was created by the "I AM" (God, the Father). The "I AM" is the authority that I came out of.

When God sent Moses to deliver the Israelites from Egypt, Moses responded to God saying, when they ask me the name of the God who sent me to deliver them, what name shall I give them? The Lord said, **"I AM WHO I AM** ... Thus, you shall say to the children of Israel, **'I AM'** has sent you" **(see Exodus 3:13-14).**

Moses was authorized ("sent") by the "I AM!" Here is what we must also understand. If we do not have an authentic identity by believing in Jesus, then authority may not flow out of our "I" (selves) as it aught. Let me explain: God is the "I AM." He then created the many "I am" (us); from the "I AM," comes us, the many "I am" (we exist); out of our existence ("I's") we were given an "identify" (the image of God).

Thus, our identity is linked to the "I AM" (God, the Father). If we understand that we are "out of" the "I AM;" and therefore, "I exist;" then I can exercise authority being under Jesus' authority. "I" (my identity, my existence) once was dead before Jesus saved me and resurrected me in spirit. Now that "I exist" out of God, I now have my correct identity,[26] therefore; I have authority under God. Do you see this?

There are many people who do not know who "they are." For some there were no natural mothers or fathers to give them an identity. Some identities were marred by abuse (sexual abuse, verbal abuse, physical abuse, spiritual abuse (flirting with satanic things), etc.). However, "as many as received Him, to them He gave **the right (lit., authority—"I exist out of")** to become children of God,** to those who believe in His name: who **were born,** not of blood, nor

---

[26] Dr. Myles Monroe has an excellent teaching on identity. Please also refer to my book You Exist! (Understanding Your Identity)

of the will of the flesh, nor of the will of man, but **of God (John 1:12-13).**

Through, faith in Jesus 'I exist" "out of" God, being "born ... of God." I now understand my correct identity. "I" do "exist" in the image of God through Jesus. That is, I now know that "I exist," authorized to become a child of God. I am under God's authority and can function authoritatively in my identity. From the "I AM" to my "I" (my "identity" from God), "I am" fruitful, "I am" multiplying, "I am" filling the earth, "I am" subduing the earth, "I am" dominating **(Genesis 1:26-28).**

"We are complete in [Christ] who is the Head of all principalities and authorities." Our identity is now "complete" in Christ. His authority now flows "out of" the fact that "I am" ("I exists"). I submit under God's authority; therefore, I can exercise authority as God has distributed to us. Finally, I must also add that power (ability) cannot work without authority.

Luke 10:19, NIV: I have given you authority to trample on snakes and scorpions and to overcome all the power of the enemy; nothing will harm you.

There is a difference between "power" ("dunamis") and "authority" ("exousia"). Power (ability, miracle) cannot work without authority. Jesus gave His disciples "**authority** ... to overcome all the **power** of the enemy; nothing will harm you." The apostle Paul exceptionally exemplifies this when he encountered a serpent on the island of Malta.

In Acts 28, after a shipwreck, Paul and the crew ended up in Malta. Paul gathered a bundle of sticks to make a fire. A viper came out of the bundle of sticks because of the fire and bit Paul on his hand. Paul merely shook the serpent off in the fire. Here is an example of showing that some power cannot affect without authority. The serpent had the power to bite Paul and release venom. However, because Jesus gave us "authority to trample on snakes ... and to overcome all the power of the enemy," the power of the snake bite did not affect Paul. The power of the serpent was nullified by the authority of Jesus that Paul walked in.

Mark 16:17-18: [17]" And these signs will follow those who believe: In My name …. [18]" they will take up serpents … it will by no means hurt them ….

The same is true in **Revelation 9.** The locusts-scorpions from the abyss have the **power** to sting and kill. However, they were only given **"authority"** over those who were not sealed[27] in their forehead. Thus, even though the locusts-scorpions have the power (ability) to sting and kill, they were only authorized over those who did not have the seal of God in their foreheads. Jesus, on the contrary, flowed in both "power" and "authority." Power worked in and through Jesus because he was submitted under God's authority.

Luke 4:33-36: [33]Now in the synagogue there was a man who had a spirit of an unclean demon. And he cried out with a loud voice, [34]saying, "Let us alone! What have we to do with You, Jesus of Nazareth? Did You come to destroy us? I know who You are -- the Holy One of God!" [35]But Jesus rebuked him, saying, "Be quiet, and come out of him!" And when the demon had thrown him in their midst, it came out of him and did not hurt him. [36]Then they were all amazed and spoke among themselves, saying, "What a word this is! For with authority and power He commands the unclean spirits, and they come out."

Jesus cast out demons with authority and power! Who gave Jesus this authority and power? God, His Father gave Jesus this authority and power. After Jesus forty days of fasting, Luke said that "Jesus returned in the **power of the Spirit** to Galilee" **(Luke 4:14).** Jesus said in **Matthew 28:18: "All authority** has been given

---

[27] There are three sealing by God: The seal of water baptism, the seal of being filled with the Holy Spirit, and the seal in the forehead with the mind of Christ. (Dr. Varner).

to Me in heaven and on earth." Jesus in turn sent us to evangelize in His authority.

Matthew 28:18-2: [18]And Jesus came and spoke to them, saying, "All authority has been given to Me in heaven and on earth. [19]"Go therefore and make disciples of all the nations, baptizing them in the name of the Father and of the Son and of the Holy Spirit, [20]"teaching them to observe all things that I have commanded you; and lo, I am with you always, even to the end of the age." Amen

Who gave us authority? Jesus gave His Church authority in Him!

Authority to Forgive

On the day when the apostle Paul was converted to our Lord Jesus Christ, one of Paul's assignments, according to **Acts 26:17-18,** was "to open [peoples and nations] eyes, to turn them from darkness to light, and from the **'authority' of Satan to God, that they may receive forgiveness of sins ...."**

Those who are under "the authority of Satan" are prevented by Satan to receive forgiveness. In other words, it is difficult for those under the authority of Satan to receive God's forgiveness as long as they remain under Satan's authority. Saying it yet another way, if you have difficulty receiving Jesus' forgiveness for your sins, you must ask the question, whose authority are you under, God's or Satan?

If you are under the authority of God, forgiveness is your portion! It follows that authority is linked to forgiveness. I may not know how you feel about this. However, I **do not** want to live under an oppressive authority of un-forgiveness! If it is difficult for you to receive God's forgiveness for your sins and iniquities, then according to the apostle your eyes need to be opened. Jesus' light must be released in your heart to deliver you from the authority of darkness that blinds your eyes.

The authority of God is the authority that forgiveness. This was one of the first truths Jesus established when He came approximately 2,000 years ago. Once, a paralyzed man was brought to Him for healing, Jesus did not immediately heal the man of his weakness. Instead, Jesus told the man his sins were forgiven to establish the truth that the Son of Man (Jesus) "has **authority** to forgive sins." In other words, Jesus asked, which is easier, to heal the paralyzed man or to say his sins were forgiven?

The obvious answer is that it is easier to say you are forgiven, than to heal a paralyzed man. Thus, Jesus healed the paralyzed man to demonstrate that if God can do the more difficult thing of healing a paralyzed man, then God can also do the easier thing of saying that your sins are forgiven you. I say unto you that if you have accepted Jesus as Savior, and you have asked Jesus to forgive your sins, your sins are forgiven, past sins, recent sins, and so on.

> [17]One day as he was teaching, Pharisees and teachers of the law, who had come from every village of Galilee and from Judea and Jerusalem, were sitting there. And the power of the Lord was present for him to heal the sick. [18]Some men came carrying a paralytic on a mat and tried to take him into the house to lay him before Jesus. [19]When they could not find a way to do this because of the crowd, they went up on the roof and lowered him on his mat through the tiles into the middle of the crowd, right in front of Jesus. [20]When Jesus saw their faith, he said, "Friend, your sins are forgiven." [21]The Pharisees and the teachers of the law began thinking to themselves, "Who is this fellow who speaks blasphemy? Who can forgive sins but God alone?" [22]Jesus knew what they were thinking and asked, "Why are you thinking these things in your hearts? [23]Which is easier: to say, 'Your sins are forgiven,' or to say, 'Get up and walk'? [24]But that you may know that the Son of Man has authority on earth to forgive sins...." He said to the paralyzed man, "I tell you, get up, take your mat and go home." [25]Immediately he stood up in front of them, took what he had been lying on and went home praising God (Luke 5:17-25, NIV).

I reiterate, Jesus demonstrated that if He can do the harder thing of healing a paralyzed man, then He can do the easier thing of forgiving our sins. "**But that you may know that the Son of Man has authority on earth to forgive sins....**" Yes, when we are under the authority of Jesus; He has authority to forgive our sins! With that said, Matthew account of the same event provided some more information. In Matthew account, the people that saw and heard the miracle that Jesus performed and the forgiveness that Jesus gave the man also understood that "men" in general have authority to forgive and authority to heal.

> Matthew 9:1-8: [1]Jesus stepped into a boat, crossed over and came to his own town. [2]Some men brought to him a paralytic, lying on

a mat. When Jesus saw their faith, he said to the paralytic, "Take heart, son; your sins are forgiven." [3]At this, some of the teachers of the law said to themselves, "This fellow is blaspheming!" [4]Knowing their thoughts, Jesus said, "Why do you entertain evil thoughts in your hearts? [5]Which is easier: to say, 'Your sins are forgiven,' or to say, 'Get up and walk'? [6]But so that you may know that the Son of Man has authority on earth to forgive sins...." Then he said to the paralytic, "Get up, take your mat and go home." [7]And the man got up and went home. [8]When the crowd saw this, they were filled with awe; and they praised God, who had given such authority to men.

Yes! Men in general have authority to heal sicknesses and forgive sins. "They praised God, who had given such **authority** to men." Thus, the principle that the Catholic priests' practice is not necessarily wrong. When they ask people to come to confession and then they forgive those people it is not necessarily wrong as long as the priests are under God's authority. Jesus also established this principle with regards to the authority of apostles.

John 20:21-23: [21]So Jesus said to them again, "Peace to you! As the Father has sent Me, I also send you." [22]And when He had said this, He breathed on them, and said to them, "Receive the Holy Spirit. [23]"If you forgive the sins of any, they are forgiven them; if you retain the sins of any, they are retained."

Wow! Jesus has "given such authority **to men,**" the authority to forgive sins or to retain sins. Jesus commissioned the disciples of Jesus. As he commissioned them, He indicated that they are to receive the Holy Spirit; and He also authorized them to forgive the sins of others or to retain sins of others depending on the situation. This is part of apostolic authority. Apostles of that day and apostles of today have the authority to forgive sins as Jesus directed, or the authority to retain sins as Jesus directed. Dr. Varner stated that the Lord told him that "He [the Lord] would deliver His creation through forgiveness." The Lord wants us to always forgive us if we confess our sins to Him. This is seen in the anointing that Jesus received.

Luke 4:18: The Spirit of the LORD is upon Me, because He has anointed Me to preach the gospel to the poor; He has sent Me to heal the brokenhearted, to proclaim liberty to the captives and recovery of sight to the blind, to set at liberty those who are oppressed

Jesus was and is anointed to forgive. The verse above reads in the Greek as such: "The Spirit of the Lord is upon Me, because He anointed Me ... to proclaim 'forgiveness' to the captives, and ... to 'send in forgiveness' them that are 'shattered to minute particles.'" Sometimes, forgiveness is the first order of business. Jesus practiced this and as "Papa Varner" stated the Lord said that "He [Jesus] will deliver his creation through forgiveness."

Those who are "captivated" by Satan or humans need forgiveness. Why? Most people blame themselves for their captivity. Thus, they need to know that that Lord also forgives them. Those who are "shattered" need to also know that they are forgiven. Why? Again, most people blame themselves for their circumstances! Thus, they need to know that they are forgiven also.

Jesus was sent to deliver us from the authority of Satan and to translate us to the authority of God that we may receive the forgiveness of sins! Jesus then commissioned His disciples with a similar authority to forgive or retain sins. Jesus later called Paul to do the same. He called Paul to "turn [peoples and nations] from darkness to light and from the **'authority' of Satan to God, that** they may receive forgiveness of sins ...."[28]

---

[28] See my book Forgiven 490 Times for more understanding concerning forgiveness

It is Finished in Him!

Hebrews 4:3: For we who have believed do enter that rest … the works were finished from the foundation of the world.

John 4:34: Jesus said to them, "My food is to do the will of Him who sent Me, and to finish His work."

John 17:4: I have glorified You on the earth. I have finished the work which You have given Me to do.

John 19:30: So, when Jesus had received the sour wine, He said, "It is finished!" And bowing His head, He gave up His spirit.

Hebrews 10:12, KJV: But this man, after he had offered 'first'[29] sacrifice for sins for ever, sat down on the right hand of God.

Jesus finished the work that the Father sent Him to complete. This "finished work of Jesus" was truth that I first heard from Dr. Kelley Varner. I must admit I could not quite implement the concept in my everyday walk when I first heard it.

Jesus finished the work! We must believe His Word and see the finished work from His perspective—the heavenly places in Christ. That is, Jesus finished the work on the cross, through His **first** and only sacrifice of Himself. He is now seated on the right hand of the Father; and we are seated together with in heavenly places "in Christ." Thus, being "in Christ" also means that all the Jesus, the Christ, accomplished on our behalf is realized on our behalf because we are in Him through baptism into Christ .

We must now cease from our own fleshly efforts and earthly ideas with regards to any previous defeated or sinful weaknesses and walk "in" the headship (authority) of Jesus Christ. Our old life is dead being crucified with Christ. Thus, we must do Jesus' work without the consciousness of weaknesses due to the old man (the

---

[29] Greek: "mian"-first

old sinful weak nature, or the ancient sinful nature passed down from the first Adam). Those of us who believe that Jesus is the Christ have been born and "imaged" with a new nature. We must now **"set our 'disposition' on things above** and not thing on the earth" **(Colossians 3:2).** As long as we understand that we are "in" Jesus, then we should think and walk in His finished work, by doing what He did as God wills.

We do not have to struggle to walk in the authority of Jesus; because we are "in Him" and the work is already completed in Christ knowing that Jesus is "given all authority upon heaven and earth **(Matthew 28:18**)! Yes, we are now part of the corporate Christ through the Holy Spirit and endowed with the authority that is in Christ, Jesus **(1 Corinthians 12:12, Matthew 28:18, Revelation 12:10, John 12:31, John 16:11).** We "are complete in Him," having been filled with the Spirit of the Lord.

In **Colossians 2:10,** most of the translations of this verse say we "are complete in Him." In addition, as indicated in a previous chapter, the Greek rendition in the Majority Texts (Byzantine Texts) of over 5,000 manuscripts and the Alexandrian Texts (also known as the NU Texts), and the Received Text (Textus Receptus) all read: "You are in Him having been filled who is the head of all principality and authority." This verse is linked to the finished work of Jesus. Because we are now **"in"** Jesus, if we are **"filled,"** the work that Jesus finished, we can now walk in the authority of His finished work.

That is, through "the authority" that Jesus' possesses, and Jesus holds "all authority;" we can also flow under the authority of His headship being "in Him." It is written, **"All things are yours .... All are yours."**[30] Jesus finished the work; He is the Head of all. Therefore, all we must do is "use speed" to cease from our own labors and enter into His headship and rest in His finished work, in which creation has been "deputized" to serve God's sons and

---

[30] 1 Corinthians 3:21-22

daughters **(Gensis 2:1-3, Hebrews 4:3-5).** "For **we who have believed** do enter that rest" **(Hebrews 4:3a).** "Let us therefore **be diligent (lit., use speed)** to enter that rest" **(Hebrews 4:11).**

Jesus finished His work and "destroyed the work of the Devil" **(1 John 3:8).** Let us use speed to cease from dead works and enter His rest. Jesus "disarmed principalities and 'authorities'" **(Colossians 2:15).** So, why should we rearm them with non-working words? Jesus "washed us from our sins," "delivered us out of the authority of darkness by translating us into the kingdom of Jesus, the Beloved Son; and therefore, the spirit Death or the spirit Satan has no authority in us **(Revelation 1:5, Colossians 1:13, Romans 6:9).**

"There is therefore **now no condemnation** to those who are **in Christ Jesus,** who do not walk according to the flesh, but according to the Spirit" **(Romans 8:1)**. We are free from the law of sin by the higher law of the Spirit of Life in Christ Jesus [the law of sin being understood to mean that sin established a law that when wan wants to do good, evil is present **(Romans 7:21)]; and Jesus freed us from this law of sin (Romans 8:2).** Jesus "judged" the sinful ruler of this world **(John 16:11);** and the prince of this world has "not one thing" in Jesus **(John 14:30). Thus, Jesus is stronger than Satan in all things!** It follows, we do not give the**(Ephesians 4:27)** Devil place!

Jesus finished the atonement and "all things are delivered to [Jesus] by [His] Father" **(Luke 10:22).** "All authority has been given to [Jesus] in heaven and on earth" **(Matthew 28:18).** "At the name of Jesus every knee should bow, of things in heaven, and things in earth, and things under the earth" **(Philippians 2:10).** All of the above is true to the fact! Therefore, we can witness in the power and authority of Jesus' headship in his "Sabbatism."

Hebrews 4:3-4: [3]For we who have believed do enter that rest … the works were finished from the foundation of the world. [4]For He has spoken in a certain place of the seventh day in this way: "And God rested on the seventh day from all His works."

Hebrews 4:6-7: ⁶Since therefore it remains that some must enter it .... ⁷again He designates a certain day, saying in David, "Today," after such a long time, as it has been said: "Today, if you will hear His voice, do not harden your hearts."

Hebrews 4:9-11: ⁹There remains therefore a rest (lit., "Sabbatism" [31]) for the people of God. ¹⁰For he who has entered His rest has himself also ceased from his works as God did from His. ¹¹Let us therefore be diligent (lit., use speed) to enter that rest, lest anyone fall according to the same example of disobedience.

There you have it! In order for us to walk in the finish work of God's rest (the "Sabbatism" Jesus accomplishes at the cross); then we must "cease from our own works" and effort. We must cease from our negative thoughts. We must rest in "who" Jesus is and "what" Jesus finished for us. Here is an assertive statement, **"some must** enter [His rest]!"

"Must" means "it is necessary as binding." It is binding that some enter His rest. Will you be a part of that "some?" The answer is Yes if you are "in Him." "For the Son of God, Jesus Christ, who was preached among you by us ... **in Him was Yes.** For all the promises of God **in Him are Yes,** and **in Him Amen,** to the glory of God through us" **(2 Corinthians 1:19-20).**

Jesus is the Head of all; therefore, we rest in the finished work of His headship; because we are "in Him." Because we are "in Him," we have already entered into His finished work! As long as we are "in Him," as He is the Head of all, we are also "lords of all," as "heirs of God" being "joint-heir with Christ" **(Galatians 4:1-7, Romans 8:15-17).** Jesus finished all the work of the Father; Jesus freed us from the orphan mentality. Thus, we walk in Jesus' victory. We walk in Jesus' finished work on our behalf. With that

---

[31] "Sabbatism" also includes, but not limited to, resting in God's finish work from the foundation of the world in which our heavenly Father deputized all creation and angels to provide for (attend to) humanity as the heavenly Father wills it.

said, we should also exercise Jesus' authority from the place of paradise, which place is in the Eden of God, the place of "up here," or the "third heaven." Per **Revelation 2:7, 2 Corinthians 12:2-4 and Genesis 2:9,** the Paradise of God where the Tree of life is located is the "third heaven." **Ezekiel 28:13** states that "Eden is the garden of God," which is different from the garden God made for Adam "in Eden."

If follows that **before** the Father created Adam and placed him in the garden, the "heavens" and "the earth" that was created together were completed **(Exodos 20:11)**. Again, the Eden of God existed **before** Adam was made. However, the heavenly Father also **"planted** a garden eastward **in** Eden," **after** Adam was created. That is, the Father finished a place (a garden withing His garden) for Adam in the third heaven (Eden, the garden or paradise of God).

He then "took" (translated) Adam to the garden in Eden; and Adam was "put" (lit., "allowed to stay") in the garden. The garden that the Father planted in Eden was the heavenly place from whence Adam "stayed" to rule the earth. Adam was supposed to be fruitful, multiply, replenish and ruled from a heavenly place in Eden, the place His pleasure.

Thus, before, the Father caused us to abide in Jesus; Jesus finished the work of His Father redeeming mankind. Jesus "through the blood of His cross … reconcile all things to Himself … things in earth or **things in heaven"** (Colossians 1:20)! The third heaven, in which Mr. and Mrs. Adam sinned, is also reconciled through Jesus' blood. Yes, Adam sinned in the garden God made for him **"in"** Eden, the third heaven. Access to the place of Pleasure, the third heaven, the Holy of Holies, has been "consecrated" (lit., "renewed") through Jesus' sacrifice (Hebrews 10:20).

Thus, we now "sit together in the heavenly[32] places in Christ" **(Ephesians 2:6).** Christ who is now "at the right hand [of the Father] in the heavenly places" has been seated "far above **all** principality and 'authority' and 'power' and 'controller,' and every name that is named, not only in this age but also in that which is to come; and He put all things under His feet and **gave Him to be head over all things to the church" (see Ephesians 1:20-22).** We now rule through the finished work of Jesus from the heavenly place, which is a prepared place in the third heaven, as Mr. and Mrs. Adam ruled from the garden God made for them in Eden.

The Father wants us to rule in His Pleasure ("Eden") through the finish work of Jesus. We are now "highly favored" by God through the Beloved Jesus **(Ephesians 1:6).** We are now His beloved ones also! In fact, **Revelation 4:11** in the Greek reads: "You are worthy, O Lord, to receive glory and honor and power; for You created all things, and **'through' Your 'pleasure'**[33] they exist and were created."

I remember during the first years of my salvation; I became sick. I remember getting on my knees asking the Father to heal me of the sickness. After I prayed, immediately I felt the warm, pleasureful and comforting love of the Father surrounding my body and I was immediately healed. It was so immediate, I was surprised!

Up to that point I had never felt His pleasure of love or to be loved like that. The feeling of His love is almost unexplainable, except that it is warm and filled with such sense of pleasure and comfort; and this same love He poured out for this world through Jesus' sacrifice. We exist through His pleasure, and we were created

---

[32] Heaven is a literal place and God created heaven and the earth together (Exodus 20:11). However, heaven can also be realized "in the Spirit;" or being "in the Spirit" is being "in heaven" (Revelation 4:1-2 with Romans 8:9, Revelation 1:10).

[33] Greek: "thelo," will, pleasure, inclination

through His pleasure. I felt that pleasure of His love in my body another time when I was resisting God's direction.

At the time, I was in the USMC on a field mission in Puerto Rico. I was due to get out of the military after my second tour; and the Spirit came to me and asked me to stay in the military. I did not want to stay in the military and resisted the Father that whole night as He was comforting me. In my resisting Him, He surrounded me with His love the entire night as I twisted and turned the whole night rejecting His request. His love that surrounded me that entire night was so wonderful, sweet, and comforting through my ordeal.

Another season in my life, in the early 2000s, the Father also allowed me to sense and smell the pleasure of the Garden of Eden. That is, for about three months; I could literally-spiritually taste the sweetness of Eden. In the Spirit, I could smell the pleasant smell of the third heaven; and the feeling of the pleasure of Eden in my spirit was so soft words cannot express properly. Again, this pleasure of the third heaven is almost unexplainable. The Word of God declares that we were created through His pleasure. We exist through His pleasure. Through Jesus, the Father has also prepared a place of pleasure for us in the third heaven, **"in Eden."**

Note: Adam sinned in a garden, Jesus was betrayed in a garden; and Jesus was crucified in a garden.[34] Finally, in Him, in Jesus, the Father has finished the work; and He has restored us to His Paradise, the garden of pleasure. Yes, we are **new creations** **"through His pleasure;"** and **"we exist" "through His pleasure."**

The Father has also "predestined us to **adoption (lit., "placing") as sons** by Jesus Christ to Himself, according to the **good pleasure** of His will" (Ephesians 1:5). The Father has also seen it fit to "renew" our access to His **garden in Pleasure—"in Eden"** (Hebrews 10:21, Revelation 2:7). In this Eden or Paradise, Jesus, our heavenly Head sits and rules in all authority. Yes, Jesus is the Head over **all** to the

---

[34] Genesis 3; John 18:1-2; John 19:41 as taught by Dr. Kelley Varner

Church! Through Jesus, we are now "the head and not the tail" **(Deuteronomy 28:13)!** How is this true?

Jesus is the Head over **all to the Church**! We, His Church, are "in Him," therefore all things are subjected to His Church. We are "in Him, having been filled with the Holy Spirit of Him who is the **Head** of all principalities and authorities" **(Colossians 2:10).** "And He put all things under His feet and **gave Him to be head** over all things **to the church,** which is **His body,** the fullness of Him who fills all in all" **(Ephesians 1:22-23).**

With that said, here are some of the "in Him" that He has finished for us.

1. He chose us **in Him before** the foundation of the world **(Ephesians 1:4).**

2. **In Him** we have redemption through His blood **(Ephesians 1:4).**

3. "**In whom** also, having believed, you were sealed **(Ephesians 1:13).**

4. "**In Him** all things 'are held together'" **(Colossians 1:17).**

5. "**In Him** all the fullness should dwell **(Colossians 1:19).**

6. We are "rooted and built up **in Him**" **(Colossians 2:7).**

7. "**In Him** dwells all the fullness of the Godhead bodily" **(Colossians 2:9).**

Finally, let us look at the finished **(the "first," and "the finished")** sacrifice of Jesus, with animal sacrifices abolished forever.

Hebrews 10:12-18, KJV: [12]But this man, after he had offered 'first'[35] sacrifice for sins forever, sat down on the right hand of God; [13]From henceforth expecting till his enemies be made his footstool. [14]For by one

---

[35] Greek: "mian"-first

offering he hath 'finished'[36] forever them that are sanctified. [15][Whereof] the Holy 'Spirit' also is a witness to us: for after that he had said before, [16]This [is] the covenant that I will make with them after those days, says the Lord, I will put my laws into their hearts, and in their 'deep-thoughts' will I write them; [17]And their sins and 'lawlessness' will I remember no more. [18]Now where 'forgiveness' of these [is, there is] no more offering for sin.

Yes, the finished sacrifice of Jesus gifts us with God not remembering our sins anymore and no future need for offering and sacrifices for sin! Let us walk under the authority of God's Son, Jesus, the Christ, our Lord Jesus!

---

[36] Or, matured

Other Books

- Poiema, by Judith Peart
- Wisdom from Above, by Judith Peart
- Identity, Sex and Your Healing, by Judith Peart
- 100 Nevers, by Judith Peart
- The Shattered and the Healing by Judith Peart
- The Lamb, by Donald Peart
- Jesus' Resurrection, Our Inheritance, by Donald Peart.
- Sexuality, By Donald Peart
- Forgiven 490 Times, by Donald Peart w/Judith Peart!
- The Days of the Seventh Angel, By Donald Peart
- The Torah (The Principle) of Giving, by Donald Peart
- The Time Came, by Donald Peart
- The Last Hour, the First Hour, the Forty-Second Generation, by Donald Peart
- Vision Real, by Donald Peart
- The False Prophet, Alias, Another Beast V1, by Donald Peart
- Son of Man Prophesy Against the false prophet, by Donald Peart
- The Dragon's Tail, the Prophets who Teach Lies by Donald Peart
- The Work of Lawlessness Revealed, by Donald Peart
- When the Lord Made the Tempter, by Donald Peart
- Examining Doctrine, Volume 1, by Donald Peart
- Exousia, Your God Given Authority, by Donald Peart
- The Numbers of God, by Donald Peart
- The Completions of the Ages, the Gate, the Door, and the Veil, by Donald Peart
- The Revelation of Jesus Christ, by Donald Peart
- Jude –Translation-Commentary, by Donald Peart
- The Better Resurrection, the Person, the Event, and the Age, by Donald Peart
- Manifestations from Our Lord Jesus Christ by Donald and Judith Peart
- You Exist! (Understanding Your Identity) by Donald Peart
- The New Testament Dr. Donald Peart Exegesis
- The Tree of Life, By Dr. Donald Peart
- The Spirit and Power of John, the Baptist by Dr. Donald Peart
- Is She Married to a Husband? by Donald Peart
- The Ugliest Man God Made by Donald Peart
- Does Answering the Call of God Impact Your Children? by Donald Peart
- Victory Out-of-the Beast-the Harvest of the Earth by Donald Peart
- Melchizedek by Donald Peart
- Ezekiel-the House-the City-the Land (Interpreting the Patterns) by Donald Peart
- Butter and Honey (Understanding How to Choose the Good and Refuse Evil), by Donald Peart

CONTACT INFORMATION:
Crown of Glory Ministries
P.O. Box 1041 Randallstown, MD 21133
donaldpeart7@gmail.com

www.ingramcontent.com/pod-product-compliance
Lightning Source LLC
Chambersburg PA
CBHW022124280326
41933CB00007B/527